HOW

DIVORCE

A

NARCISSIST

AND

WIN

MARIE SARANTAKIS

 ADRIKOS, LLC

Oak Brook, Illinois, U.S.A.

ADRIKOS, LLC

ADRIKOS, LLC | Oak Brook, Illinois, U.S.A. | www.adrikos.com

Library of Congress Control Number: 2021911678

Publisher's Cataloging-In-Publication Data
(Prepared by The Donohue Group, Inc.)

Names: Sarantakis, Marie, author.
Title: How to divorce a narcissist and win / Marie Sarantakis, Esq.
Description: Oak Brook, Illinois : ADRIKOS, LLC, [2021]
Identifiers: ISBN 9781737393399 (paperback) | ISBN 9781737393313 (hardcover) | ISBN 9781737393306 (ebook) | ISBN 9781737393375 (PDF) | ISBN 9781737393344 (ePub) | ISBN 9781737393337 (mobi) | ISBN 9781737393351 (Nook)
Subjects: LCSH: Divorce—Law and legislation—Popular works. | Divorce—Psychological aspects—Popular works. | Narcissists—Psychology—Popular works.
Classification: LCC K695 .S37 2021 (print) | LCC K695 (ebook) | DDC 346.01/66-dc23

Cover Design by MiblArt

Disclaimer: This book is not intended to serve as medical, psychological, or legal advice. You should not use it to diagnose or treat any conditions. If you or someone you know is suffering from any psychological or medical impairment, you should seek the assistance of a licensed physician, psychologist, and/or mental health provider. Always consult with a licensed attorney in your jurisdiction to determine any legal course of action applicable to your specific situation. The content contained herein is for informational and educational purposes only. No liability is assumed for losses or damages due to the information provided. You are responsible for your own choices, actions, and results. This book should not be utilized as a substitute for professional advice.

To my narcissist.
You probably think
this book is about you
(and it is).

CONTENTS

INTRODUCTION

Divorce sucks. Even under the best of circumstances, it is hell. For those who have been married to a Narcissist, you have experienced the Ninth Circle of Dante's Inferno... the very layer where Satan himself resides with Judas. Ironically, Dante refers to this level as the "pit of treachery." It is where the betrayers of special relationships are entombed in a frozen lake of ice. Quite fitting for the Narc, because that is precisely what they do: They betray those closest to them. They sinisterly love inflicting pain on those who love them. Their hearts are frozen. Their souls are made of ice. No doubt about it: You have experienced an evil like no other.

Now here is the good news. While it may not feel like it, you *will* prevail. There is one way, and one way only, to beat the Narc. That is to have him or her suffocate in their own miserable game. If you are in a divorce, whether by choice or circumstance, leaving them is the only way to reclaim your soul and drown the Narc in their own poison.

As a divorce attorney, I witness countless cases of narcissistic personality disorder. Sometimes it is my client's spouse who is afflicted. Sometimes it is my client themselves. However, it was not until I experienced this breed of evil up close and personal that I knew how to handle it in the courtroom. It is often either unidentified or misdiagnosed. This book will help you determine whether you were married to a Narc, understand what happened to you, teach you how to deal with the Narc in the courtroom, and finally how to rebuild your life post-divorce.

So let's begin our journey.

CHAPTER 1

Welcome to Narcland

If you are reading this book, you are probably utterly confused. You are desperately searching for answers. *What just happened? Does my ex really have narcissistic personality disorder (NPD)? Is that even a real thing? What causes it? Can they get better? Will I ever get better? How do I move on? Did they ever love me in the first place? Do I have it, too?* Then you wash, rinse, and repeat those same questions over and over again in a vicious cycle, trying to reconcile in your mind how the person you cared for the deepest of all, the one who purported to be your soulmate, is now your enemy.

It makes no sense. You are doing what any reasonable and healthy person would do: trying to understand the whirlwind that just occurred. You are never going to get answers from the Narc themselves. That is what makes this process even more painful.

Let me reassure you. You are not alone. This book will help you identify and understand what just happened to you. You'll have your doubts at times, but ultimately a sense of peace will finally wash over you. A peace that you haven't felt in years.

You may have thought that during the periods of time when the Narc "love bombed" you that you felt peace, but you didn't. Intuition is deep. You were living in a constant state of fight or flight. Perpetually walking on eggshells in fear of losing what you thought you needed the most. That is the irony of being with a Narc. They are what gives your soul unrest, and yet they convince you that they are the antidote.

NPD is real. It destroys lives. Not just the life of its host, but all of those with whom the host comes in close contact. It is a disease that plagues our society in huge numbers. Unlike other diseases in which the victim is a bystander to an unfortunate circumstance, NPD is a disease that one chooses to have and derives pleasure from. Your spouse makes a conscious decision each and every day to be rotten. They can stop at any time, but they choose not to.

Despite their affliction, you have become addicted to them. You have become dependent on serving their needs, and they make you falsely believe that they fulfill yours. The Narc takes you on a rollercoaster ride of emotions until you become physically and mentally exhausted. You live in a perpetual state of fear and anxiety. You become accustomed to living in underlying unrest. You do everything in your power to keep them happy, and it works for a little while, but it never lasts. In fact, the more you placate them, the more they get off on the high of bringing you back down.

You convince yourself that you are helping an emotionally distraught soul find solace; all the while, they are eating away at you, and you don't even know it. Instead of fixing them, you find yourself begging for them to fix you, trying so hard to regain even crumbs of the attention they once gave you so freely. Crumbs are exactly what you'll get. Little treats here and there. Just enough to keep you clinging on until you no longer serve a purpose to them. That's when they'll dispose of you. If you leave in time, you will only have some emotional scars. If you wait too long, you will likely be physically and financially depleted as well.

Do you remember the sweet old days of love bombing? When you thought you had found your one and only? When you wondered how someone so perfect could actually exist? When you believed everything you had ever dreamed about had finally arrived? The reason it felt so intoxicating is because the Narc is an expert at reading others. They study you like a book. They learn your deepest desires and hone in on your reactions. They are so attuned to reading even the most imperceptible emotion on your face, that you will be convinced that the two of you are completely simpatico.

They take this extreme interest in you so that later they can manipulate and gain unshakeable control over you. The Narc does not feel or get attached. Because they are hollow inside, they become hyper-observant in order to replicate authentic behavior. They perform with precision, because reeling you in is a sport. Initially, they take on every single quality they believe you want them to have. Then they ultimately become a reflection of you. They pretend to share the same goals, passions, and ideologies. The two of you are the only ones who really understand each other. They make you believe that it's the two of you against the world. That way you shut everyone else out. You don't need anyone else. You have the Narc. They listen to your every word and cater to your every need. You are smitten. Meanwhile, they are just taking notes.

During courtship, the Narc will confess their undying love to you at what will feel as though it is a very strange, and maybe even inappropriate, time. It's usually very early on in a relationship. Your instinct would tell you that this person cannot truly be in love with you, not yet at least, but you want to believe it. You have your doubts, but you silence them. You don't want to ruin what could potentially be the very best thing that has ever happened to you. You become very good at silencing your inner voice.

This other person is so enchanting, that even though you have your doubts, you get lost in the fantasy. If the Narc senses you are resisting falling for them, or fail to respond by gushing in kind, he or she will do everything in their power to prove their devotion is genuine. They will shower you with countless gestures and never-ending attention. They will be affectionate and doting. You become the very center of their universe. Everything they do revolves around being with you. They remember the little things you say. They show up in unexpected places to surprise you. They plan your futures together. While you believe they are genuinely addicted to you, it is all a ruse carefully crafted to get you addicted to them.

Normal people do not engage in love bombing when they meet their soulmate. They realize that love is a serious commitment with real responsibilities and repercussions. To the contrary, they are more cautious of moving too fast because they do not want to jeopardize a good thing. Narcs just view love as a plot twist. They confess their undying devotion early and often. It will seem artificial. Too soon. Too strong. That's because it is.

This is a common tactic of predators. You'll likely get a flood of text messages during the early part of the relationship. Narcs love text messages. There is a special charge they get texting you while doing something else entirely contrary to what they are communicating. For example, they may be texting you about how much they miss you and can't wait to see you tomorrow. All the while, they may be sitting at the dinner table with another paramour, rolling their eyes, telling them that you will not leave them alone and are obsessed with them. It gives them a real rise to live double lives. They love to appear as though they are being stalked and in high demand.

After a continued period of love bombing, constant attention, and affection, you will eventually be convinced that their devotion must be true. Clearly, their actions match their words. Yet, in your gut, something still tells you this is wrong. You sense it, but you do not want to believe it. Maybe it's just nerves. You tuck your fear away, convincing yourself it's just silly old insecurity. After all, none of your past relationships have worked out, so maybe you just don't have the imagination to think this one can last either. Perhaps you should give this one a chance. You shudder even thinking about the possibility that this could end one day, so you refuse to believe it. Your guard continues to go down as time goes on.

As you share more intimate conversations with your Narc, they tell you about their past loves. None compared to you of course. They talk about their psychotic ex who was much too into them. That is a common thread. They emphasize how they were highly sought after and prized. Then they infer how their exes pale in comparison to you. They conclude by sharing how their ex wronged them in some unfortunate way: withholding affection, tricking them, breaking their heart, taking all their money, alienating their children—the list goes on and on. The story changes each time, but, rest assured, the Narc was the victim of a cruel ex-lover. Listen closely to whatever they accuse that person of; they are usually guilty of that very thing themselves. It is also what they will later accuse you of doing when they discard you—deflection is a common tactic of sociopaths.

You pity them. You think, *How could anyone not treat this man or woman like the royalty they are?* You cherish how lucky you are that the ex did not recognize your partner's incredible attributes. Over time, the Narc will continue to tell you more stories about their ex. They'll probably eventually share that one or more of their exes are still chasing them. They feign how annoying it is to be so desired. It's great marketing on their part.

Then, out of the blue, they start talking about their ex's positive attributes. You become confused. You justify it by thinking that your Narc is just being completely and totally open with you. They do this intentionally so that you will start to feel in competition with their ex. You fear losing them. The ex, if nearby, may even resurface. You may find yourself feeling a bit concerned, a little self-conscious perhaps. It's normal for even the most confident person to have insecurities when it comes to the intimate relationships that they hold most dear.

Then your Narc starts to disappear now and again. They go from constantly monitoring your every breath to making you wonder why they abruptly stopped. If you inquire, they say you are needy. They set the pace of giving you constant attention because they want to make you seem unhinged when it suddenly goes away and you start to ask questions. They start to test the boundaries of what gets a rise out of you. It's all going to be used shortly to make you look clingy. Just wait.

You quickly realize these disappearing acts are not worth mentioning. You know that normal human relationships do not require constant reassurance, but you can't help but feel very uneasy when these events occur. *Where are they? Are they doing this on purpose? Have they met someone else? Are they with their ex? Did I do something? When is it okay to text? To call? To stop by on a surprise visit? Are they ever going to contact me? Did their phone battery die? Did they die? Am I overthinking this?* Your mind starts to race. You start yearning for some contact to put your mind at ease. Then you get it. All is well. Until the next time.

These mini disappearing acts become more and more frequent. No matter how cool you play it, the Narc knows it eats away at you. They can smell fear. Uneasiness is their oxygen.

You start to question the Narc. Subtly, of course. They become inflamed, and then they punish you for daring to question their behavior. They do this so that you become fearful. They control you. You don't control them. How dare you try.

They need to teach you that lesson, but how? Easy: by increasing the bouts of ignoring you. This is usually in the form of the silent treatment. They want to make you feel as though you are not even worthy of any explanations. Nothing messes with a person's head more than another person not willing to engage them. It is demeaning and annihilistic. The person choosing not to engage, or allow the conversation to proceed, is the person who is in control. The Narc will never waste an opportunity to passive-aggressively tell you that they are in charge.

Eventually, you apologize. You don't even know for what. You just want the intolerable silence to end. You need some affection. You need a hit of your drug. Once you come crawling back, they will give it to you. And all is well. At least for now.

This cycle repeats over and over and over. The more you succumb to their expectations and demands, the less respect the Narc has for you. The gifts, the attention, the dinners—all begin to dwindle once the Narc knows they have you. They consider their time to be extremely valuable, so they are very cautious about how they expend their energy. Once they believe they have you all in, they begin looking for a new supply. Wasting precious effort on you is futile. You're already putty in their hands, and they know it. They are off to conquer something and someone else.

One way that the Narc gains control over you is through marriage. This is a commitment that is not easy to break. Narcs do not get married because they are madly in love, want to spend the rest of their lives together, and raise a family. They get married because that is what they are expected to do, and as a byproduct they gain more control over you. It feeds into the narrative that they are desired and perfect. Almost every action a Narc takes is either for appearances or control. Marriage serves both ends. After the wedding, their mask starts to slip. They start to expose more of their rotten attributes. They know they can get away with more than ever.

Despite a high number of Narcs going through the divorce courts, Narcs detest the idea of divorce. They find it altogether unnecessary. They should be able to carry on multiple lives while you take care of the house and children. Rules apply to you, not to them. They want you to stand by their side and take the abuse. They don't look at you as a partner, but rather as someone who owes them a duty. They may amuse themselves with you so long as you have something to offer: attention, social status, kids, money, praise, you look good in the Christmas card photos, etc. It's not because they made a commitment to you. The only thing a Narc can be loyal to is themselves.

As time goes on, they continue to deplete you of whatever it is that you are giving them, until it is no longer fun for them. Once they know they have you fully hooked, the joy of being in the relationship continuously decreases. They may still play some games with your mind for sport in order to entertain themselves. One of their favorites is gaslighting. The Narc loves to make you think that you are going crazy. They make up events that never happened and deny your recollection, as though your memories are entirely faulty. They move things around and hide them from you. They change minor details in stories to make you think they have a better memory than you do. They convince you to doubt your own mind and rely on them instead.

During gaslighting, the Narc wounds and soothes you. They are the poison and the antidote. They go from cruel to caring in a flash, resulting in you not being able to reconcile what is happening. *Are they good or are they bad? Do they love you or do they hate you? Are they your partner or your enemy? Are you that flawed? Are they just trying to help you?* You feel lost, and they are feeding you misinformation.

All the while, you are either making them look good or providing for them in some way, whether it be work, the house, or taking care of their personal needs. You spend so much of your time keeping them happy, that you forget what makes you happy. Even if you remember, you won't have time for it. The Narc keeps you completely preoccupied meeting their needs. Before you know it, you find that your life revolves around catering to them, even when they are not present. They continue to be around you less and less, but you spend more and more of your time satisfying their needs. You'll be chasing your own tail trying to take care of them, to please them, and to keep them happy. To a Narc, the world revolves around them, and they will eventually convince you to believe that, too.

One day, without rhyme or reason, they seemingly lose interest in you. Like an old toy, you're no fun anymore. You have no idea it's coming. Like a little child, they meander off the playground, and you are left alone, completely and utterly confused. You realize they are not emotionally vested in you. You grow fearful they may one day leave you altogether.

Narcs often temporarily check out of the relationship during special occasions. You could be in the middle of a vacation. It could be right before an incredible anniversary. Narcs love to destroy anything that is intended to be dear to you. They despise anything that takes the attention away from them, and they hate to see you filled with joy. That childlike innocence you bring to these momentous occasions makes the Narc angry. Yet it is one of the things that attracted them to you in the first place. They feel a need to pretend to live in a perfect storybook, but they are incapable of feeling that sense of joy and hope; therefore, they must maim it in others. They feel robbed of that type of wholesome pleasure, and the only thing they can feel is the diabolical joy that accompanies the control of taking it away.

If there is a celebratory occasion, you can count on them showing up late. Of course, they'll have a good reason: Work. Traffic. Something innocuous. Do not be fooled. This delay is intentional. How can they be the center of attention if they arrive at the same time as everyone else? They always need to stand out. If being late doesn't make sense, they pick a fight or have a general sense of melancholy so that those closest to them can't help but feel completely oppressed and guilty for having a good time.

The Narc slowly steals everything out of your life that once gave you pleasure. Before you know it, you have become their lackey, and they look at you as a drain. They put you down and then build you up. They speak down to you in an infantile and derogatory manner in private, but remain complimentary about you in front of others. While they used to be generally upbeat and have a positive disposition, they are now almost always in a foul mood. They even seem to blame you for it. You keep trying to make them happy. You desperately fight to bring back the person you fell in love with. It works. Just for a little while, though. Then they go back to treating you like the servant they think you are.

If you're smart, you'll walk away, not ask any questions, and never come back. But if you're like most of us, you'll want some answers. You'll give them another chance. In fact, you will give them many more than they deserve. The Narc may give you some mild love bombing as a treat, less and less each time, and only as much as absolutely necessary to keep you around.

You plead for some reprieve from the oppressive cloud that now looms over the Narc, beg for the way things used to be, and try to win your way back into the Narc's good graces for a brief period of solace. The Narc gives you some excuse: How tortured they are. How you drove them to their behavior. How you are the only one who understands them. They then thank you for giving them another chance. You believe that they are remorseful and miss you. You are grateful that your family will remain intact. *It was just a phase*, you think.

Simultaneously, the Narc is securing his or her new supply and preparing to deliver a final blow—the discard. A bigger and nastier breakup than the ones before. They aim to make it humiliating and degrading. It empowers them to think they have destroyed you. It makes them feel god-like. Discard does not mean divorce. It just means they are removing themselves from you. Maybe it's physically. Maybe just emotionally. The distance is impalpable. You panic. You don't understand what happened. Why did they shut you out? Do you stay and take the abuse? Do you try and cure the defects in the marriage? Or do you walk away? You question and doubt yourself at every turn.

Narcs do not like to be the ones who initiate divorce proceedings. They would much prefer that you silently stand by and let them do whatever they please. They consider it absurd that you expect them to be monogamous or to supply you with anything at all. Rules apply to you—not to them. You give. They take.

Divorce does not fit into their description of being the perfect spouse. The Narc tries so desperately to curate this wholesome image to the outside world. Sometimes, however, their desire to punish you far outweighs their need to appear as the ideal partner. Plus, if they sense that you are somehow disparaging their reputation, they will ensure that they draw the line in the sand. The Narc filing for divorce is the exception and not the rule. The Narc will file first only to save face or if there is some tangible benefit for them to do so. Even then, they hate being the ones to pull the trigger. They don't like to overtly cause conflict. Their chaos is much more passive-aggressive. That makes it much easier to feign being the victim.

By staying married, the Narc can also continue to exert total control of the money. That is why during the marriage they give their spouse just enough to keep them content. Not enough to have any freedom, though. Once the courts are involved, they are no longer in charge. Narcs don't like to share, and they certainly don't like anyone telling them what to do.

More often than not, it is the Narc's spouse who decides that they finally have had enough of the Narc's abuse. They realize that there is no hope in rectifying a marriage with someone who is so profoundly broken and has no desire to change.

This phase goes on for months. Sometimes even years. You may be in this phase now. Vacillating whether to stay or go. Even after filing for divorce, you may wonder whether you should give the marriage another chance. You may contemplate going to therapy together to try to salvage all that you have built. Even if the relationship is imperfect, you convince yourself that it is worth giving it another chance. You are torn. The idea of staying away and leaving is equally terrifying. You talk to the Narc to get some clarity. They sense your inner struggle and take advantage of the opportunity to work their way back into your world. Narcs hate therapy, but they very often are willing to go. Not because they are sincerely interested in reconciliation, but rather because this is another opportunity to regain control.

Marriage counseling sessions soon turn into a stage where the Narc tries to convince the therapist that you destroyed the relationship. Pay close attention. What they tell the therapist is what they are telling other people as well. They pretend to be receptive to implementing the therapist's recommendations, but nothing really changes once you leave the office. You try to explain to the therapist that these suggestions do not apply to your situation. The therapist insinuates that you are not trying hard enough. Meanwhile, it is the Narc who is impeding any meaningful progress. They hide it well by paying the therapist lip service. The Narc pretends to give great reverence to the therapist's sage advice. It looks like you are the one who is refusing to work on yourself. The Narc has twisted the story yet again. You can't even get a word in. You start to dread going to therapy. The Narc is so crafty at controlling the dialogue. You find yourself defending your behavior even when you have done nothing wrong. You accept that the marriage is really over. The Narc has revealed themselves as a con artist yet again.

Once you realize that you have been taken by the Narc the entire time, it all starts to make sense. The puzzle pieces come together. You replay moments in your mind, but now the things that once seemed disjointed have an explanation. One of the bizarre things about Narcs is they all exhibit the same temperament. They may be crafty, but they are not original. When you read about the other cases out there, it's as if they are all the same man or the same woman. It is uncanny and mind-boggling. *Do they read a handbook? How do they all play the same series of sick games with menacing tricks?*

It turns out that the person who you believed to be one-of-a-kind was actually just a textbook Narc. Nothing about them is remotely unique. The story of your relationship was spelled out before it even began. They sabotage the people who love them the most, and they do it in the exact same way. Take solace that once you identify them, you can predict their next move. You will no longer find yourself mystified by their behavior. By knowing your opponent, you can outsmart them at every turn.

While it hurts, you need to know: They never loved you. They are utterly incapable of it. The reason it felt so good to fall for them is because they are masters at mimicking love. It seemed perfect because they can only give you romance out of a movie. They don't know what love really is, so they replicate the over-the-top gestures and passion that they witness on the big screen. They don't act based on their feelings; they act based on how they think you want them to.

You fell in love with yourself. You told the Narc who you were and what you were looking for, and they became that person in order to draw you in. You now not only have to deal with the loss of the Narc, but the loss of the fantasy. You realize that your hopes and dreams were built on a lie. This other person took advantage of you. You were all in, and they were never vested at all. It's the ultimate betrayal.

NPD is not just a personality disorder; it's a morality disorder. Narcs have no desire to abide by the boundaries of what is right or wrong, because everything is relative to them. Good and bad are defined by what satiates their desires at any given moment. They lie, cheat, and steal. Then they blame you for the fallout. They manipulate you until they break you and then get angry at you for your weakness. They only feel alive when they hurt you. To cause pain is to have control. Narcs aren't crazy; they're cruel. They are 100 percent aware of the evil masterminds that they are, which is why they try so hard to mask their personas.

Not all abuse leaves a scar. Emotional abuse is just as real and can be just as damaging as that which is physical. The abuser can hide themselves and even convince the victim it is all in their own head. Because emotional wounds do not leave visible marks, no one on the outside can see the pain being inflicted on you. No one intervenes. You often question whether it really occurred.

Emotional abuse usually starts off rather trivial. Maybe they follow you, demand instant responses, patronize you, and make you doubt your recollection. These things may seem annoying, but not insidious. The problem is, as the relationship develops, the abuse worsens.

Over time, the Narc compromises any relationships that you have with others. They make you grow solely dependent upon them, all while playing the role of your savior. Once they feel they have sufficiently alienated you from your previous support structures, they begin to exhibit fits of rage. Their weapon is their words. Sometimes the lack of words, the silent treatment, can feel just as crippling. Masters of charm and manipulation, they won't be satisfied until you're mentally broken and reduced to a shell of your former self.

That is the irony: The Narc is an empty shell devoid of any emotion or ability to feel. The chaos they inflict through constant gaslighting and invalidation is designed to bring you to the same fate. You find that the core of who you once were becomes slowly erased with ongoing abuse. Being with a Narc means becoming increasingly numb for self-preservation. Your personality and ability to feel slowly wither away until you are a cheap replica of your former self.

Narcs are perpetually bored. These games they play, bringing you up and down, are for sheer sport. They live in their own heads, and when things begin to grow stable in their environment, they grow weary and pull some stunt to inflict pain and generate new amusement. Sometimes they create a fight for absolutely no reason at all and without any provocation whatsoever. They cause chaos because it gives them control. You will never feel safe or at ease with a Narc. They'll make sure to remind you of that the moment you express any comfort. They get their high by keeping everyone around them on pins and needles. The Narc lives in their own reality show where they are both the protagonist and the producer.

You may wonder: How can someone who seemingly loves you treat you this way? Easy. Narcs don't love; they use. Narcs live in their own little make-believe world: Narcland. Everyone else in their story is just a dispensable extra. An actor can stay in the story so long as they remain obedient and serve their role as a faithful sidekick, ultimately making the Narc look good. Even if they remain loyal to the part, at some point the Narc will get bored and swap them out for someone new.

The Narc's life is a vicious loop: different supporting actors, same game. Every relationship they are in will have the same fate; the only question is how much abuse the other person is willing to withstand before they get off the ride and what state they are in when they finally do.

CHAPTER 2

Defining Narcissistic Personality Disorder

The term "narcissistic personality disorder" (NPD) is somewhat of a misnomer. When people hear the word "narcissist," they mistakenly assume it simply refers to someone who has an inflated ego. In general conversation, a narcissist is someone who is all about themselves. Someone who suffers from NPD is actually much more deranged and sinister. To differentiate your everyday narcissist from someone who suffers from NPD, this book refers to the latter as a "Narc." A narcissist has a deep love of themselves, whereas a Narc also has a deep hatred for others. All Narcs are narcissists, but only some narcissists rise to the level of Narcs.

Narcs treat those who love them in a predictable manner. They repeat predatory behaviors compulsively with different characters in the soap opera that is their lives. They reserve their most vile attributes for those who are closest to them.

Failed relationships caused by one partner being selfish are common, so how do you know whether you are involved in a relationship with a Narc? A key tell is that your partner went from treating you as though you were gold to being altogether repulsed by your very presence for no reason whatsoever. Narcs engage in insidious cruelty that defies logic and leaves you feeling worthless.

If you are wondering whether your spouse suffers from NPD, ask yourself whether they engage in any of the following behavior:

- Exaggerate their accomplishments
- Respond to criticism with rage
- Treat those closest to them the most poorly
- Preoccupy themselves with visions of grandeur (including power, success, and beauty)
- Engage in gaslighting
- Obsess over their looks
- Resort to the silent treatment
- Manipulate and belittle others
- Show off their material things (including flashy clothes, cars, and homes)
- Believe others are envious of them
- Fixate on winning at all costs
- Experience frequent and unexplainable mood swings
- Switch personas depending on who is in front of them
- Become infuriated if someone questions their authority
- Lack empathy for others
- Micromanage their environments and everyone around them
- Pair themselves with partners who appear as a trophy
- Demand to be treated better than others and have a sense of entitlement
- Require constant attention and admiration
- Monopolize conversations

▶ Struggle in close interpersonal relationships

The Narc is a discrete type of sociopath. To the outside world, they are charming, charismatic, successful, sweet, and considerate. In the privacy of their home, they are controlling, cagey, deceitful, selfish, and manipulative. Many of their negative traits and unhealthy preoccupations mean that they achieve great success in their professional endeavors. They have a tight grip on their environment and are not distracted by catering to the needs of others. They are solely fixated on their own well-being and success. Their obsession in making themselves appear larger than life results in them quickly climbing up the corporate ladder. The Narc is ruthless with a smile and has an insatiable need to run the show. Their personalities are best suited for a high-level management position with little supervision, such as a doctor, lawyer, or entrepreneur. Narcs are natural leaders because they know how to control everyone around them.

While appearing wise and even-keeled on the surface, the Narc has the emotional maturity of a petulant five-year-old child. They throw tantrums and are infuriated by seemingly mundane transgressions. You are confused by the trivial things that fluster them and ruin their day. Meanwhile, major life events occur that others perceive as devastating, but the Narc carries on without missing a beat.

It terrifies you a bit. You realize that the Narc's reactions to things are often inappropriate. The moody and dark Narc who lacks normal emotional regulation is such a stark contrast from the idyllic person that you fell in love with. You are perplexed trying to reconcile these seemingly two different beings. Rather than questioning the Narc's behavior, you question your perceptions. You are always receiving external validation from the outside world that your spouse is praiseworthy. You excuse their behavior. Maybe they are just stressed. As time goes on, you start to see this other side of them come out more frequently, especially in private.

When out and about in the community, the Narc always presents well. They are charming, attractive, and goal-oriented. They conform to the dictates expected in their elevated social circles. They surround themselves with an elite pedigree of acquaintances, because they delight in associating with other powerful and wealthy people for status. Many are actively engaged in civic organizations, not because they believe in any particular cause, but rather because they love receiving acclaim. The Narc strives to be the quintessential model citizen. Recognition validates their superiority. While they are constantly receiving praise from strangers for their wonderful attributes, their families often witness a starkly different person behind closed doors.

Narcs usually succeed in fooling people because the average human being cannot comprehend that someone can be so callous, calculated, and cruel. They want to believe in the Narc's inherent goodness. It is hard to imagine that someone can be so fake. The Narc doesn't ever really get close enough to other people for them to be exposed. They have countless acquaintances, but very few, if any, close friends. They would much prefer having a fan over a companion. They struggle with the idea of anyone being their equal. This is why intimate relationships are so tumultuous for them.

Narcs go through the following cycle with their significant others: (1) Love bombing (2) Devaluation (3) Discard (4)

Hoovering. These stages repeat incessantly until the victim wises up and leaves or is left feeling utterly broken, destroyed, and worthless. This pattern provides the Narc with comfort, but, more importantly, it is designed to give them unwavering control.

Everything that they do comes down to control. Once you understand that, you have the Narc figured out and can anticipate their next move. While the core of NPD boils down to power, some Narcs are very stealth (covert) while others are more grandiose (overt). Both are equally as dangerous, but they go about it in different ways.

The Covert Narcissist: This type of Narc is subtle, rather than bombastic, in their disposition. They thrive on pretending to be a victim or hero for attention. Therefore, they are more challenging to readily identify. They often appear sensitive and are prone to depression if their true nature becomes discovered by others. They have a strong desire to appear kind and helpful. However, just like their overt counterparts, their intentions are rooted in power over empathy. Appearing righteous can be a very crafty tool for manipulation. Covert Narcs can hide their NPD for a very long time. Even those closest to them may not be certain whether they are dealing with a Narc.

The Overt Narcissist: The overt Narc is extroverted. They openly relish being the center of attention. They have no qualms telling you that they are the best. Remarkably, while appearing to be the life of the party, they are anti-social. This Narc knows how to work the room while not meaningfully connecting to anyone. They must dominate every situation they are in. If things do not go their way, they become unstable and easily enraged. This type of Narc is much bolder and therefore easier to identify.

Regardless of which type of Narc you are dealing with, they feel most alive when they are receiving supply. "Supply" is another word for attention. They are not satisfied with plain old regular attention, though; they need total submission and admiration from those around them. Whether it is a room full of people or their home environment, they cannot get enough veneration.

That is why Narcs typically have two love interests at a time—a primary and a secondary supply. Narcs have learned they cannot depend on anything, so they often need two of everything. It's a security thing. As a bonus, they play the two individuals off of each other to get a bigger fix. Oh, how the Narc loves people vying for their attention. The Narc makes each person believe that the other is the villain, and if it weren't for the other person, they and the Narc could live happily ever after. This is a common triangulation tactic.

Even though Narcs struggle with interpersonal relationships, they almost always get married. They are obsessed with conforming to societal norms and rejoice in the idea of appearing desired. Yet it's this very normalcy that they later grow to resent. They are not subject to rules. The fact that they are supposed to be monogamous with one partner for the rest of their lives makes them angry. They start to resent their spouse for having such an expectation.

Narcissistic men, often, but not always, are misogynists. Many have a twisted and deep-seated hatred for women. They see women as either saints or harlots, and sometimes the same women will transition into both depending on what purpose she is serving in the then-moment in the Narc's life. Their propensity for adultery, coupled with their utter lack of respect for women, means that they enjoy degrading the women they are with and then further punishing them with infidelity.

If you are with a misogynistic male Narc, he tells you that all women are crazy, but that you are the exception to that rule. You are so unlike the other women in his life. You are different. You are special.

Don't worry: You'll soon fall from grace, too. The Narc already has their worldview; they are just waiting for it to be convenient for you to conform to it.

Female Narcs are addicted to power and see men as nothing but objects. They are a means to an end. Comply with their demands, or else. They will alternate from being the sexy femme fatale vying after your attention to treating you as some pathetic loser who is expected to cater to their every whim. They are only concerned about their own needs being met. They seduce you only to abuse you.

Female Narcs also more frequently resort to martyrdom as a tool for manipulation. They suffered so dearly, therefore they deserve to be recompensed for their sacrifices. They endured hardship for you, and now you must repay them for all that they gave you. Nothing you do will ever be enough.

Keep in mind that these patterns are gross generalizations. Not all male or female Narcs neatly fit into these categories. No matter whether they are male or female, all Narcs are hypocrites. They create rules of conduct, but the moment you comport with their demands, the rules shift. You find yourself chasing after an elusive, nonexistent goalpost. Of course, you should never expect them to abide by the same rules that they set for you. They believe that they are the herder; you are the sheep.

The Narc believes they have a right to control you. They may even have the audacity to tell you it's for your own good. The Narc provokes you to the ends of the earth and then chastises you for speaking up about their abuse. All the while they pretend to be calm and above the fray. They do this by giving you the silent treatment.

While insufferable at times, the silent treatment is still better than the alternative. Their other modus operandi is throwing a tantrum completely disproportionate to the magnitude of the issue at hand. They default to straight-up intimidation and bullying. They become absolutely distasteful if something doesn't go their way. Narcs are irresponsible and impulsive. When they fight, they never play fair. They say and do the things that hurt you most.

While they act as though they are the beacon of morality in a lost world, they intentionally inflict pain on those closest to them. They are con artists who target their inside circle for victims. Even ordinary thieves have limits. They usually can't steal from those with whom they've formed personal bonds and share close connections. Narcs precisely target taking from those closest to them. They steal your time, money, love, affection, and innocence. If they believe that you have betrayed them in any way, they will show you no mercy.

Whatever deplorable traits they have, they immediately project onto someone else. For example, Narcs frequently refer to others as being bitter. All the while, there is no one angrier at the world than the Narc. They are particularly repulsed by happy-go-lucky personality types and feel the need to teach everyone a lesson about how life really works. They spread pain and insecurity on those dependent on them. The irony is that they are drawn to happy, empathetic, and courageous people: the very traits that they lack.

They were drawn to you because on some level they want to *be* you. You exude all the things they wish they could naturally possess. They start to take on your personality and mimic you. They realize that society perceives these things as good and so desperately want to portray themselves as such. Inevitably they will later resent you for your wonderful disposition and temperament and try to deprive you of that goodness.

The Narc will eventually abandon you. Deep down you know that. You convince yourself that if you behave a certain way, you can stop it from happening. You live in a state of fight or flight. No matter what you do, they will leave you, and not just once. They will leave and reenter your life many times. It's much more painful that way.

When they check out of the relationship, they won't just disappear into the abyss. That would be much too merciful for their liking. They will come in and out of your life as they see fit. Their attempts to get you back are referred to as hoovering. The moment you pay them any mind in return, they accuse you of being obsessed and controlling. You cannot win if you continue to engage the Narc. You can only win by getting as far away from them as possible. But they make that incredibly hard to do.

The unfortunate theme that so many survivors experience repetitiously throughout the course of an NPD relationship is the constant waiting. They put their lives on hold for the sake of revolving their schedules around their narcissistic partners. They wait for the Narc's mood to be just right. They wait for the next random fight. They wait for things to get better. They wait for the inevitable discard they know is coming. This constant waiting game creates an unshakable anxiety. You can't live a normal life, because you can't get off the hamster wheel.

As the discards increase in length and frequency, and you become more resilient to their transgressions, the Narc looks for new opportunities to inflict greater trauma. They love to abandon you when you are going through something difficult. If you experience a tragedy, you can bet they will proverbially kick you when you are feeling down. If you expect them to display any patience or empathy towards you, they will become irate. They are annoyed that you could even make such a request. Their reactions to something negative happening to you, whether minor or catastrophic, is perplexing. You will be utterly confused by their cavalier response to your bad fortune. They may even get mad at you for being upset.

Why does the Narc get mad when bad things happen to you? For starters, you are going out of character. Your role is to support them. Secondly, you are shifting the attention to you, which to them, is a direct affront. To the Narc, emotion is only good for manipulation, so they get angry, thinking you are trying to get something over on them. Flat tire? Death in the family? Illness? How dare you! What kind of stunt are you trying to pull? You're going rogue and off-script in the Narc's sitcom.

Never forget that a Narc is a predator. They target the good and the innocent. They capture their prey in their web.

They abuse and defile for pleasure—luring in their victim with false promises and shiny gifts and separating them from their friends and family while keeping them emotionally captive in a sick and twisted case of Stockholm Syndrome.

They destroy those who come close to them and deny it until the day they die, playing the saint and the victim. The harm they do to those who love them is an atrocity. At one point, they may have been a victim of some unfortunate circumstance themselves. Some Narcs can't stop reliving the vicious cycle of hurt that they experienced in their past, and instead of working through their own trauma, they transpose it on others because it makes them feel powerful. It gives them a sense of control that they never had in their own lives. If they cannot regulate their own emotions, they can take refuge in the fact that they can control yours. There is no intimacy, no caring, and no love. It is all about manipulation and control.

Even though the Narc makes you feel so low, they chose you because of your strength. Narcs are not attracted to weak people. They are drawn to those who are magnetic, attractive, intelligent, and caring. The question is not why they chose you, but rather why you would ever choose them.

No one ever knows they are marrying a Narc. No one in their right mind would sign up for that. The Narc is a chameleon who appears to be the perfect mate. They can hide their off-putting qualities for years. The Narc could win an Oscar for how well they can feign sincerity. By the time you realize what has happened to you, you are often at a place where it's no longer that easy to walk away. Maybe you no longer have financial independence. Maybe

HOW TO DIVORCE A NARCISSIST AND WIN ■ MARIE SARANTAKIS

you share children together. Maybe you have isolated yourself from your family and friends. The person who treated you like royalty at the onset of the relationship is a far cry from the monster who you find yourself married to today.

30

CHAPTER 3

Love Bombing

It all starts with the love bombing. Out of nowhere, you meet the love of your life. This feels so different from all of your past relationships. A euphoria like no other. You are a giddy teenager in puppy dog love. Physically and emotionally, you are bonding with the Narc. They whisper sweet nothings in your ear. They surprise you with bold gestures. They incessantly confess their undying devotion. Fabulous trips, romantic dinners, gifts for no reason, and never-ending conversations about nothing. You can expect excessive communications at this stage of the game: good morning texts and constant check-ins. It's not needy; it's adorable. It's not intense; it's thoughtful.

The initial love bombing stage can last for weeks, months, or even years. The Narc keeps up this charade however long they believe it is necessary to snare you. To the Narc, love is a tool for manipulation. They dole it out like a drug.

When a drug dealer is trying to get a subject hooked on their poison, they provide them with their first hit for free. It is a little taste of the dark side, a seduction of how good it can feel to be under the influence. They create a dependency. The recipient accepts the drug, believing they can quit at any time, but they can't. Eventually, they will do anything for their fix. They will destroy themselves from within just to feel alive. Love bombing by the Narc uses the same premise of addiction.

They waltz into your life and offer you everything you have ever wanted. Your vision for a future is handed to you on a silver platter. It seems too good to be true. Your gut tells you this cannot be real. You know there are risks but convince yourself that there is no harm in giving this relationship a chance. Soon you are hooked. It's ecstasy. You will do anything to keep the Narc in your life. You cannot get enough of them. You are all in.

Once you become intoxicated by the Narc, everything else in your life pales compared to getting your high. Their affection is incredibly powerful. You destroy yourself and everything you love just to have your Narc by your side. Your emotional well-being becomes regulated by them, and you can no longer function without your "narc"otic.

It's so easy to get caught up in the rush. The early stages of a relationship with a Narc are exhilarating. This time period is the strongest weapon in the Narc's arsenal to keep you tethered to them when things later deteriorate. Throughout the relationship, even when things eventually take an ugly turn, they regress to love bombing whenever necessary to pull you back in.

During the love bombing stage, the Narc is actively working to strip you of your independence. They get you to commit to small and innocuous things in order to increase your level of devotion to them. Eventually, after they build up enough of your trust, you find yourself agreeing to things that make you uncomfortable. You hand over control. Make concessions to keep them happy. They start making all of the decisions, but they falsely make you believe that you consented to their authority.

You are not concerned about these things though. You are absolutely smitten. You obsess over spending as much time with them as possible. You won't listen to anyone else who tries to warn you that you no longer seem like yourself. In fact, you are likely angry or annoyed if they do. You don't want to know the truth. You repress the feeling in the pit of your stomach, because you don't want the other shoe to drop. You push aside any uneasiness you have, knowing that this is all too fast and too much. No one else gets you quite like the Narc does.

The Narc refers to you as their soulmate. Every song reminds them of you. They never really experienced love until they met you. You are so much different and better than their psycho ex. You believe them. Common sense tells you to be cautious of those who get too close too quickly. The narrative they feed you tells you that their love for you is the exception to all other rules.

Sociopaths don't work their way into your life by revealing themselves as the cold-blooded, selfish monsters that they really are. They do so by appearing kind and endearing. Evil always comes in disguise. The Devil doesn't win people over by showing his horns. He does so by pretending to be everything you ever wanted so that you forsake everyone else around you to give in to the temptation. They are the forbidden fruit in the Garden of Eden.

The Narc comes to you in the form of the most beautiful, charming, sweet, and charismatic human being you have ever met. As masters of manipulation, they play up to your specific wants and needs. The Narc, while emotionally stunted themselves, has an uncanny ability to know what others want to hear. They are a bloodhound sniffing out your deepest desires and conforming themselves to match the description of your ideal mate. They pretend as though their entire world revolves around you. It's flattering and hard to not get caught up. You are drowning with copious amounts of attention, affection, and praise.

It is incredibly simple for the Narc to put on this performance, because they lack an authentic identity. They mimic the personality of whomever they are focused on at that particular moment. They develop a mask. All you can see is this magnificent human being who is much too good to be true. They are everything you've been looking for in a soulmate for your entire life, but that's only because they are taking your cues and emulating anything you desire. They may parrot your mannerisms and your work ethic, feign your interests, and pretend to be engaged in your hobbies. It's all a façade.

You didn't fall in love with the Narc; you fell in love with yourself. Your deepest dreams and desires were realized in front of you. You were duped by someone who was pretending to be your perfect match and subsuming your identity. You are your own soulmate. You are what made that relationship so beautiful. You are the one who brought everything to the table. This fake persona that the Narc carried out while in a relationship with you is one that you created. They studied you and became who they thought that you wanted them to be. Narcs mirror people. You need to understand that the Narc was never that person. That person is actually you. Don't ever lose yourself to a cheap replica of yourself again.

This is why, eventually, when the Narc moves on, they seem to be a completely different person. The person you thought you knew, didn't ever exist. It was a carefully designed ruse that was created while they wanted to appease you. The moment the Narc is no longer trying to win you over, they are off mimicking someone else. That is the stranger you see at the end.

It is so easy to fall hard for the Narc. They are charming, slick, cunning, and engaging. Their words are poetic and their ability to cater to your fantasies is uncanny. They have a grandiose idea of themselves and act as if they hold you in an even higher regard. You start to believe that the two of you can take over the world. While normally we detest arrogance in another, the narcissist knows exactly how to distract you. They convince you that they are highly prized but the only thing that they desire is you. They pretend to hold you in an even greater esteem than they hold themselves. You become so flattered by the compliment that you completely overlook their overtly braggart behaviors. Next thing you know, they are boasting about how great the two of you are together. United you can do anything. You are the dream team. A power couple. You complete each other.

Rather than revealing how obsessed they are with themselves, the Narc pretends to be completely captivated by you. They want to know everything about you. Your hopes. Your dreams. Your fears. All things they intend to use to later lure you into their web and control you. If you want to know the core of what drives the Narc, it's control. They don't have it over themselves, so they must have it over others. Anything you say and do will soon be used against you.

Narcs have a number of tricks they use to draw you in. One common ploy is that they make you privy to fake secrets. They tell stories that begin with, "I've never told anybody this before. ..." There will be a huge buildup, with a letdown of a story. They typically provide you with confessions of things that really don't matter, but they pretend that you are the only one who knows. That's because the story itself is irrelevant. They are seeking the feeling that it provokes. Their fake divulgences are designed to make you feel connected and vulnerable. You think, *They must be a good person if this is really the worst thing they have done.* You begin to feel obligated to share things in return, things that you have never shared before. You almost feel like you owe it to them. They opened up to you, so you should reciprocate. You find yourself caught off guard. The Narc intentionally does this so that you will share things that you have never shared with any other person. There are two primary reasons for this. First, it makes you feel even more connected to them. Second, they later have things to hold over you whenever it strikes their fancy.

Another stunt is that the Narc likes to throw around the words "I love you" early and often. They do so because it means nothing to them. If they say it enough, they know that they can convince you to believe it. They drive an hour out of their way, just to find you, give you a kiss, and tell you they miss you. *How could anyone who put in that much effort be faking it? How can it not be true love?*

The Narc puts in an extraordinary amount of work in on the front-end because they know it will pay off later. There are no limits to what a Narc will do to ensure they get you hooked. Bold gestures are commonplace. They would risk everything just to have you. It's a movie kind of love: love that you thought did not really exist in real life. That's because it doesn't.

The overarching theme is that the Narc cannot get enough of you. They want to be with you constantly. They revel in making plans with you, whether it be dinner or growing old together. Since you are going to be together forever, why not intermingle your finances? They will try to move in on your financial situation and pretend as though it is a sign of their commitment to you. They make it seem harmless. For example, maybe the Narc buys something with you, and they are the one who pays for it. What harm is there in that? The harm is that they will eventually gain more and more control over everything you owe and own. Once they gift you something, they expect more in return. Most of all, they expect your reliance on them.

You throw caution to the wind despite your better judgment. Eventually, you've been playing the role of spouse for so long that you agree to marry them. It's just a piece of paper. Might as well make it official. You are so caught up in planning your future together that you don't recognize what is happening in the present moment. The Narc is selling you on the most beautiful fantasy of what forever will look like. They need to prove to you that they are all in. There is an inundation of attention. The pleasure centers in your brain are firing off like crazy. To the Narc this is a game.

For you it's about love. For the Narc, it's about control and appearances. They look at marriage as ownership over you. Plus, it fits into their narrative. They want to seem perfect on the outside. There is a societal expectation that they have a stable home environment and family. You fit the role. If they remained single, they may appear undesirable. Marriage is not about building your lives together; it's what they are supposed to logically do next.

The stronger you are, the longer the Narc needs to keep you suspended in this state of pleasure before you agree to wedded bliss. The Narc will not move on from this part of the game until they are completely and utterly convinced that you are spellbound. Once they know they have you, that is when the mask will start to slip. It may be before you walk down the aisle, or it may very well be several years later.

The Narc is not in a rush to move to the next stage of their manipulation. They know the longer they keep it up, the more they can get away with later. Besides, love bombing is fun for them as well. Even if they are incapable of attachment, it can still be a good time to go through the motions of being in love. The Narc has this innate fear they are not good enough, so they enjoy the constant affirmation that you give back in return. They enjoy going through the process, but unlike you, they never develop a meaningful connection.

Narcs need constant attention. This is often referred to as "narcissistic supply." Love bombing is a good way for them to receive supply and validation. They are insatiable. No matter how much praise they receive, or control they have, it will never be enough. Seduction is a powerful game, and they are the masters.

While this is most euphoric stage of the relationship, it's also when the Narc is the most malignant. During this period, they test your boundaries. They constantly push you outside your comfort level, feigning whatever course of action they are encouraging you to take as being in your best interest. They do this to measure how far you will go to comply with their requests and create fear bonding.

You perceive the Narc's actions as protecting you. Just like when your parents encouraged you to grow outside your comfort zone, it seems strangely familiar when the Narc does the same thing. Don't fall for this false comfort. The Narc is not looking out for you. They do not have your best interest at heart. They are merely testing your boundaries and getting you comfortable with compliance. The more they can get you to do outside your comfort zone now, the more control they can exert over you later.

At some point the Narc will become preoccupied with your whereabouts. They want to know what you are doing and who you are with at every given moment. They are jealous and insecure, often admitting it, and using these flaws as a compliment to feign being fearful of losing you. You are flattered. It's cute. You begin to think they can't live without you and are only acting this way because they are so afraid of losing you.

You slowly become deprived of every sense of privacy you once had. They likely are using some sort of tracking device and/or camera to monitor you, and you willingly allow them to do so. The ironic thing about the relationship at this stage is that they are abusing you and you enable them to do it; but you have no idea you are being abused. It's disguised so well. As the Narc becomes you, your identity also morphs into that of the Narc. You no longer know any boundaries. Your two worlds have melded into one. Nothing they do feels like a violation; rather, it feels romantic. You don't think much of it. After all, even the Bible says that "the two shall become one flesh."

After the Narc knows they can control your location, they will begin to control your schedule. The Narc will discourage you from pursuing your own interests. In extreme cases they cut you off financially, blackmail you, guilt you, or take away your mode of transportation. Pretty soon your world becomes the mock reality of what it once was with the limitations they have imposed on you. Because you are showered with love and praise, you don't even realize that it is happening.

The Narc eventually cuts you off from your family and friends. They consume all of your time and claim they want you all to themselves. When you spend time with anyone else, they either insert themselves under the guise that they so deeply care for you that they want to be a part of every facet of your life, or they keep you so busy that you do not have time for anyone else. Their love is all-consuming. They pretend that you are their entire world, so that you feel obligated to reciprocate in kind. Before you know it, you go from being a successful independent person to fetching their laundry. Rather than being sad about losing yourself, you enjoy being their gopher. That is how sick and twisted this manipulation is.

Eventually, the Narc succeeds in cutting you off from all of your support systems to make you completely and utterly dependent upon them for approval, emotional support, and direction. By breaking off your connections to the outside world, they invariably make themselves the center of your world. Plus, they avoid anyone else from catching on to what they are doing to you. They don't want anyone else alerting you to the fact that you are the victim and that they are a predator.

Down the road, when they finally decide to cut you off from their life altogether, you come crawling back, because they are all you have left. The Narc can make the most independent person completely codependent. Their goal is to work you into an obsessive frenzy, completely caught up in the relationship. By pretending to be obsessed with you, they are conditioning you to be obsessed with them. It is a complete guise.

Towards the end of the relationship, you may feel as though you have been beaten down to a shred of your former self; but this doesn't mean that you are weak. Quite the contrary. You are a strong person who is in a bad state. Often Narcs pair themselves with more successful partners than themselves. It is odd, since they have this attention complex. The game to them of bringing someone down so low, who was so up so high, is intoxicating. They enjoy the process of watching you fall. That is why they are drawn like a magnet to beautiful, thriving, and driven mates. Their partner needs to be someone with status. Keep in mind that when a Narc love bombs, they take on their partner's qualities. They only emulate someone who is, in their eyes, worthy of being imitated.

Plus, Narcs play in high-ranking social circles. They are drawn to successful partners who present an image that is compatible with their greatness. They love a trophy on their arm. Whatever society says is to be desired, that is what they want. So if a Narc selected you, take it as a compliment. You are their idea of perfection realized. Sadly, they don't believe in happy endings. That is why they need to destroy you.

They are insanely jealous of any attention, praise, or adulation you receive. Your success is a direct assault on them. Keep in mind: The Narc is all about shifting the focus on them and maintaining complete control over everyone and everything in their world. That is why they work so hard to ensure that their once independent partner becomes completely dependent on them. For example, if you have a flourishing career, they may offer to work harder so that you can stay home and raise the children. They buy into this idea just long enough for you to lose your connections, opportunities, and confidence. Then they resent you for not working while they struggle to keep you lavished in your unreasonable lifestyle. You become trapped. You gave up what you spent your life building for their sake, but they turn around and allege that they in fact are the ones who gave up everything for you.

If you even toy around with the idea of doing something for yourself, or becoming more self-reliant, they become jealous and irate, while downplaying any prior success you had. They make you feel guilty for even considering doing something that doesn't revolve around them.

You'll notice that they punish you for doing well. If you create something remarkable, it leads to conflict. If you get a promotion at work, they make you feel guilty for putting your job above them. If you are recognized with an award, they pick a fight. This is intentional conditioning to ensure that you do not excel in any way without them taking the credit. As a result, you naturally shy away from opportunities to shine, because you do not want to be reprimanded. Instead you funnel that energy into making the Narc shine. Like a bad Pavlovian experiment, you are conditioned that the only time you receive praise is for doing what they train you to do.

You may even be convinced that you do not deserve the attention and that your role is to serve them. Eventually you become completely dependent upon and subservient to the Narc by your own free will. Ironically, they need you much more than you need them. The moment they recognize they are becoming dependent on your supply, they begin to sniff around for a backup. They fear intimacy. It is almost as though they become angry at you for making them remotely vulnerable. They become livid for making them feel anything at all. The more they feel, the more distant they become, and the more they punish you for it. To deescalate the conflict and return to the sweet love bombing, you will shift your attention to the Narc's needs. They are happy again. All is well. At least for now.

In order to ensure that you don't try to find your voice again, the Narc keeps you busy as their personal assistant, so you never even have the time to think about yourself. For the Narc, it is not enough just to keep someone from achieving their potential; it's even more fun to bring someone down who was on such an upward trajectory. It's not enough for the Narc to emotionally abuse you; they must financially deplete you as well.

If you had assets and liquid cash when you met them, they will encourage you to tie up that money in some way. It is okay to spend your money on discretionary things like vacations, since the Narc promises to take care of your basic needs. It's okay for you to take your inheritance and spend it on a second home in both of your names; that way your money is tied up, and they now have control over it. It sounds like a good deal, but it's not. The promise to take care of you is only for a little while. Once you no longer have your own financial freedom, the tides change.

Because you are only a means to an end for them, they have no remorse in leaving you struggling to meet your basic needs. You have been conditioned to be fearful of achievements in your professional career, so you likely are stifled. As time goes on, you begin to lack the skills and confidence to progress to where you would have otherwise been. You now need the Narc to survive. This is when you may realize that the love bombing was never real. It was a cleverly designed ploy to get you to trust them and give up parts of yourself.

There is no horror quite like the realization that your dreams are shattered, but also that the relationship was only an illusion in the first place. You knew in your heart something was not quite right. You always had that sense of fear and uncertainty, but, despite your better judgment, you brushed it off.

Just like the Narc never really loved you, you never really loved the Narc. You can't. You don't even know them. You were in love with the idea of the Narc. That is why you were so caught up. It's difficult to abandon the fantasy.

The Narc is completely incapable of loving you or anyone else. Nevertheless, they put on a good show. A simple dinner is an Oscar-worthy performance of pulling out all of the stops. Narcs can't love, because only people who are real and vulnerable can love. They are neither of those things.

They do, however, fake vulnerability. They love to play the victim. It's a common gaslighting tactic to turn the tables. Plus, they get more attention that way. They may woefully confess how sensitive they are, traumas they've endured, and pains inflicted upon them. The "poor me" routine is a classic in the Narc's handbook. They recant scripted stories in order to elicit sympathy. They are desperate to show their emotional depth. Some go so far as to fake illnesses or mourn over deaths. These sick and twisted souls will use sympathy to gain control of you. This is all part of their carefully woven game designed to lull you into exposing your deepest and darkest secrets, which of course will be leveraged against you when the opportune moment strikes their fancy.

While at times you may doubt the monster you were with, you need to know that it was all intentional. It was a carefully crafted play where you were the love interest. Your fantasy role will soon evolve into a dramatic one. The overkill love bomb stage was designed to learn precisely what you desire, give it to you in excess, and then later withhold it from you in the devaluation stage for control.

CHAPTER 4

Devaluation

Once a Narc believes that you are fully committed and dependent upon them, they begin to pull away. This phase is a lot less fun than the last, but not quite painful enough for you to end things altogether. They still feed you with enough crumbs of love and affection to keep you hanging on, but they intersperse it with ever more frequent bouts of cruelty.

The hallmark of the devaluation stage in the relationship is confusion. The Narc's goal is to have you doubt yourself and to keep you in the dark about what they are really doing to you. They will engage in gaslighting and excuse their bad behavior by subtly blaming you for anything faulty they may have done.

Gaslighting is a form of manipulation where the victim is intentionally lied to in order to make them doubt their perception of reality. It is one of the Narc's favorite hobbies. They try to make you believe that you are foolish, inept, and make poor choices. Some Narcs take this to the extreme by attempting to convince you that you have gone completely mad. They may even suggest you need to seek medical intervention. No matter how far your Narc takes it, their purpose is always the same: to make you doubt your own abilities and therefore become completely dependent upon them for your survival.

The term comes from a 1938 play titled *Gas Light*, which was later adapted into a highly acclaimed black and white film in the 1940s. The premise of the story is a husband convinces his wife that she is plagued with mental illness. In the film, Ingrid Bergman plays a character named Paula, who marries Gregory, played by Charles Boyer. Despite her hesitation, Paula marries Gregory after only knowing him for a mere two weeks. She gets caught up in a whirlwind romance and throws caution to the wind. After they are married, he suggests they move far away. Paula is removed from all of her family and friends. For a period of time, they live in wedded bliss. Shortly thereafter, his temper begins to reveal itself and so do his devilish tricks. (Yes, Narcs have been around a long time. This is nothing new.)

In the story, Gregory's trickery starts off subtle. The more he gets away with, the further he takes it. Eventually he convinces Paula that she in entirely unwell and incapable of trusting what she sees in front of her. A common motto followed by Narcs is, "Your eyes may deceive you, but I never will."

All Narcs gaslight. It is their form of entertainment. This game is designed to make you believe that you are the crazy one. You begin to question your sanity and perception of reality, and you reassess all of your boundaries. Thus the Narc gains even greater control.

Classic gaslighting techniques include:

1. Minimizing Situations: The Narc makes you believe that you are overreacting. They do something egregious and then blame you for it or pretend that what they did was not altogether that bad. In fact, according to them, the only thing disproportionate and out of line is your reaction. This conditions you to never express your dissent. You are taught that your feelings are invalid and should be stifled to avoid conflict.

2. Denial and Misrepresentation: The Narc tells you that you misunderstood a situation or a conversation. If you ever question them about their recitation of the facts, expect an explosive response in return. You start to accept their account of reality at face value, even when you know they are incorrect, simply for the sake of not causing a fight. The more you allow them to get away with this, the more outlandish their accounts of reality will become.

3. Deflecting: The Narc is all about themselves, except when you get into a disagreement. The attention quickly shifts from what they did, to your reaction. If it's not about your response, then it is about how someone else is influencing you to act in an unflattering way. This is another tactic to distance you from others. Either way, the attention shifts from their wrongdoing onto your "inappropriate" behavior.

4. Stereotyping: The Narc may lump you into some category. "Everyone like you acts this way." They may say things like, "All women are crazy," or, "All men are jerks." This is a put-down to make you seem unimportant. You are one of the many. You are no one special. It drives home

the message that you are replaceable and is a subtle provocation to make you try to appease them and prove that you are not like the rest. Psychologically, you switch to defense mode in trying to win them over.

5. Implying You Need Help: The Narc is quick to insinuate that you have a mental or emotional defect that is causing you to lash out or not properly process information. Maybe you need anger management classes, are drinking too much, or your memory is failing you. No matter what they allege, the theme is that you are broken and need to be fixed. They are only trying to help you. You are the one causing the turmoil because you are not cooperating with them.

The gaslighting goes from delicately trying to convince you that you are mistaken about things, to downright hostility. They act as though they are taking on this hard disposition for your own good. They need to be mean to you to shake you out of this false reality you are in. Ironically, the only false reality is the one that they created. They become incredibly patronizing under the guise of concern.

When they grow bored and need a little amusement, they manufacture a situation to inflict some gaslighting. In order not to seem downright cruel, they intersperse it with the techniques they used during the love bombing stage. For example, the Narc may suggest the two of you have a romantic dinner at home together. For added effect, they'll even mention how very much they're looking forward to it. You set the table, prepare their favorite meal, and wear something special. They arrive home from work and tell you that they have already eaten. You don't understand. You put in all this effort at their urging, and they forgot? No. They'll quickly tell you how you must have misunderstood. They never suggested this. Maybe not that night. Maybe not at all. Plus, how can you be upset with them for working? You need to pay more attention. What's the big deal, anyways? You're overreacting.

Another example is that you may have enjoyed a lovely evening out on the town together. You go home, get in bed, and find them going to sleep by themselves on the couch. It was a great night. *Why are they avoiding me? What happened? Are they cheating? Should I say or do something? What caused the distance?* You blame yourself. If you bring it up, they get annoyed and insinuate you did something to cause it, or they just give you the silent treatment. You apologize, not even knowing for what. They are too disgusted to accept. They are so tired of dealing with you.

You start to realize that nothing is predictable. You doubt your own perceptions of the status of your relationship. You think, *Maybe I should try harder. Did I do something wrong? Did I misunderstand?* The sick and twisted part is that the Narc is painfully aware of your confusion. They manufactured it. From the innocuous changes in plans to their mysterious reactions, the Narc loves watching you try to figure out what is happening. They have been through this process countless times with many others. You are just another part of their story, sandwiched in between others who they will make to feel the same way. No matter how many years you have been together, to the Narc you are another cog in the wheel.

This ambient abuse creates a hostile environment laden with fear, control, and intimidation. None of the Narc's actions are overt. That way there is no proof of their abuse. They know how to keep their hands clean and appear to be perfect, kind, and generous. Meanwhile, not realizing what is happening, you are sure to leave trails of evidence showing you are crazy. Those texts of confusion, desperation, and anger that you send will be great fodder for them to share with their next victim during the subsequent love bombing stage they will enjoy with them. They will savor the content and recycle what you give them.

Anyone who experiences prolonged gaslighting is riddled with fear, anxiety, and doubt. You become a master of holding back your feelings until eventually they just pour out of you. Oh, and the moment they do—how the Narc has been waiting for that moment. That is when they make you out to seem like the crazy person. They can stab you a million times, and the moment you fight back, they sit there calmly looking at you and pointing out how unstable and insane you are. Smirking all the while. There is nothing quite like the evil genius smirk of the Narc. You start to feel guilty for expressing any emotion. You wish you had not said anything. You pray it could be undone. The next time, you hold back. You do not question them. You do not dare fight. Slowly, they take away your voice. Eventually you doubt yourself, because the only voice you hear in your head is that of your Narc, and what they may say next.

The thing is: You are not crazy. You were abused. No one who loves you could ever watch you be in pain. Once a loved one is wounded, all bets are off. Someone who cares for you will stop and comfort you, irrespective of who was wrong or right. It does not matter what the argument was about, they cannot stand to see you suffer. The Narc gets giddy watching you writhe in pain.

Your torment is their oxygen. It is a supply that not only gets them high but is essential for their very survival. If you notice that your partner is deriving pleasure from the fight, you are likely dealing with a Narc. Healthy people do not enjoy conflict with their significant others. Narcs love it.

Once you catch onto what is happening and point out any uncomfortable truth about the Narc, they get angry. Not the normal type of angry — enraged. The bigger the scene they cause, the less likely it is that you will ever bring it up again. You learn to stifle your emotions and never share how the Narc is hurting you, because if you do, they make you immediately regret it. They blame you for not only the fight, but just about everything else that is going wrong in their life at that moment.

All of the attention is taken away from their misconduct and is now directed towards you. You become engulfed in a war of words that leaves you blindsided, until you eventually end up apologizing again—but don't even know what for. You fear speaking your mind, withdraw, and internalize anything that troubles you. You just need this brutal war to end. As a result, the Narc knows that they can get away with just about anything and that you won't dare question them about it.

No matter what the Narc has done, don't ever expect an apology. They try to make you feel that anything vile they did to you was ultimately your fault. That you made them do it. Even though they can attack you ad nauseum, they try to make you feel you have no right to ever question them in the slightest. They are annoyed if you believe that you are worth an apology or their attention. They immediately redirect the focus back on to themselves, and as an added bonus, they'll throw some salt in your fresh wounds. Ironically, this confusion, while horrific, keeps you further bound to the

Narc. You get used to them defining reality. While completely unhealthy, you become ever more dependent on their whims, just trying to keep them appeased and stable.

When you dare to ask questions, you are attacked for bothering them or questioning their authority. They even become agitated and annoyed, saying something to the effect of "Oh god, here we go again." It is all part of the gaslighting, making you believe you are the difficult one in the relationship and muzzling your voice.

If you have ever been in an argument with a Narc, you know what it is like to hit rock-bottom. You tap out. What other people would consider to be normal questions, the Narc takes as a hostile affront. How dare you question their superiority, point out their flaws, or catch them on a lie?

Either you are so fearful of losing them, or they are so convincing that everything is your fault, that eventually you stop. You break down. You tell them you cannot take it anymore. You love them. It doesn't matter who is wrong or right. You beg them to stop. Instead of looking at you with compassion, they display that shallow smirk again. There is nothing more satisfying to a Narc than kicking you while you are down. They are livened by your defeat and now have confirmation that they can continue to torment you, knowing that you'll stick around and take it.

What naturally happens to a victim during this stage is they begin to suppress any statements or comments they believe may incite a negative reaction from the Narc. They will become very calculated with their words and measure every action they take so as not to cause the Narc to experience a bad mood. The irony is that the crueler the Narc becomes, the kinder the victim becomes. On the flip side, the nicer the victim becomes, the more abusive the Narc turns. The reactions are contrary to what you would expect in a normal and healthy relationship. For example, if you become overwhelmed with sadness, and begin to cry, the Narc is infuriated. They don't feel compassion towards you. They feel anger. To them, crying is a form of manipulation, it is not an authentic reaction to feelings. If a person can fall asleep at night knowing that you are crying, they don't really love you.

The Narc is the poison, but they have cleverly convinced you that they are the cure. They cause your tears, but you believe they can make them end. Even when you know they are hurting you, you have an insatiable urge to go back to your abuser. They are the only one who can make the situation right. The Narc's ability to wound and soothe is remarkable.

The abuse is so gradual at first. It is almost imperceptible. Then it escalates. Their bad moods become more frequent. When the two of you are alone, they no longer feel compelled to be charming, yet they continue to be captivating in public. You realize they just are no longer trying to impress you.

Rather than thinking something is wrong with the Narc, you start to question whether something is wrong with you. Why are they still their former selves when in public, but miserable when they are alone with you? You try harder to appease the Narc. To impress them. To get back what you had before. The love bombing felt so good, but it's becoming less and less frequent.

As time goes on, the Narc will continue to test just how deep their control runs. You mean nothing to them. You are an extra in the movie. They see your kindness as weakness, so in turn they demean you more. They find it humorous and will even brag about how they cut you off from their affection, but in classic Narc fashion. They will spin the story however it suits them and based on the audience. To their new love interest, they might say they left you for them. To the outside world, they might say they did the admirable thing and cut the crazy out of their life. They will describe you to others as if you were a cancer. You needed to be completely removed, as your presence posed a significant danger. Everyone around the Narc will start to see you as the bad guy. Even people who once cared for you will start to treat you differently. The Narc is a puppet master. They have a great hold on influencing the perception that others have of you. The more the Narc alienates you from others, the more control they maintain over defining your world.

As the Narc continues to taunt you, they figure out that no matter what they do to you, you will keep coming back. You are fighting to save your marriage. You are single-handedly trying to make things right. They know you will try to open the lines of communication even when they shut them down. You will probably say something sweet or even apologetic. No matter how hard you try to repair things, you will be met with disdain and contempt. The Narc get off on pushing your buttons just as much as they get off on watching you pine away to have the pleasure of apologizing to them. They won't actually accept your apology until they watch you grovel and break. They will only let up if they believe that they won or if they are concerned that they are losing control.

People are not that complicated. If they hurt you once, they will hurt you again. The Narc will definitely hurt you again. Your pain is their supply. They need it as much as they need oxygen. While they sinisterly derive pleasure from causing you pain, they equally enjoy bringing you back up again afterwards. Both are an intoxicating form of control. This yo-yo effect will continue to play out. With time, the Narc begins to perfect the art of giving you as little joy as possible to keep you hanging on, while maximizing the amount of punishment they inflict upon you. Breaking you feeds their soul.

In any relationship, kindness, compassion, and forgiveness are generally virtues. When you are in a relationship with the Narc, the more accepting you are, the more they will take advantage. They will intentionally violate any boundaries you have set. These ups and downs will increase in frequency. You will become addicted to the highs. The lows won't even matter anymore. You know they are temporary. Subconsciously you may even look forward to them, because you know that a period of love bombing will soon follow. Victims stay with the Narc because these lows are often followed by intense highs—never quite as good as the highs felt during the initial love bombing stage, but a decent imitation.

This isn't love. This is trauma bonding. You so desperately crave validation and affection from your abuser that you accept their behavior at all costs. This addiction is just as deep and just as real as the stronghold of an opioid. You will do anything to get your next fix, even if it kills you. The brain confuses this intensity for love. This yearning for the Narc's affection to soothe often outlasts the relationship. Even when you know that the marriage is irreparable, you still feel as though you need them.

The gaslighting that you have experienced has created a great deal of damage that has gone undetected for a long period of time. You worry that nothing that you do is good enough. You need external validation for even the most minor decision. Your confidence is shaken. You fear sharing your experience because you won't be understood. Besides, you have isolated yourself from your prior networks. What you once loved feels empty. The things that motivated you seem pointless. You struggle remembering the person you used to be.

The devaluation stage of the relationship can have some serious and lingering effects on your mental and physical health. You become accustomed to feeling unsafe. You live in constant fear that another attack is coming. You know it will be illogical. You start to change your behavior. You become more accepting of behavior you'd never otherwise tolerate in a relationship because you fear the repercussions. The Narc is aware of your fear. They can smell it. They are intentionally testing your boundaries. You may have panic attacks, generalized anxiety, and heart palpitations.

Eventually the Narc becomes tired of plain old fights. The gaslighting is boring after they prove to themselves that they can continue to get away with it. They need to up the ante. They start a new technique. Their other modus operandi is the silent treatment. They get crabby about something and then innocently state, "I'm not going to argue with you." They imply you are at fault and not worthy of being heard; they act superior and decide what will and will not be said. There is nothing crueler or more dehumanizing. It sends a message that you are not even worthy of a response. The desperation that results from intentionally being ignored or rejected is torture. By controlling who speaks and when, they win an argument that they never even have to engage in. This is a brilliant tactic designed to control both you and the narrative.

They fluctuate between the silent treatment and outright anger. The Narc gets annoyed with you for having a completely valid and normal reaction to their abuse. Maybe it's just verbalizing or pointing out something that they did hurt you. The Narcs response is to blankly stare at you, then make an expression of disgust, and then blatantly continue to ignore you as punishment for having the audacity to say anything that does not sound like praise.

As they increase the number of times they pull out the silent treatment and fits of rage, they will likely simultaneously start paying more attention to someone else. It doesn't always have to be another love interest. It can also be another family member or work commitment. After all, how can you fault them for paying attention to their child or working? Whatever it is, you will be vying for their attention. They now only give you any positive affirmation after they punish you. You subconsciously start to look forward to the lows, because it's the only way you can get their attention.

When the Narc first met you, they likely told you about their crazy ex. The ex used them and maybe even cheated on them. They were the victim. They continue to bring it up during the course of the relationship, maybe now saying you are just like their former beau. You start to pity your assailant. They aren't evil. Maybe they were abused. They treat you like this because they don't know any better. You actually believe that they are the ones who are the victim.

The Stockholm Syndrome has set in. Now it makes sense: Your Narc isn't evil, they are damaged. You'll get through this together. The Narc is a master at masking their abuse by appearing to be the victim. Somehow, they convince others that their behavior is justified. They are a good person who is fundamentally broken at the hands of another. This is another example of deflection.

All the while, the Narc is telling someone else you are doing the exact same things. This so-called crazy ex, maybe isn't really an ex at all. Maybe they are still in the picture. Maybe they'll resurface shortly to make a guest appearance and make you feel insecure. Oh, and how the Narc will get off on the joy of watching the two of you fight over them. This is what makes them feel alive. Well, this, and watching you cry.

Devaluation often signifies the beginning of a new love bombing stage with someone else for the Narc. Even if they have met their new paramour, they are not going to get rid of you completely. This is where they begin to toy with you. They cannot lose. If you have had enough and leave, they are left with their new supply. Most likely though, you stay and fight for their attention. This makes the Narc feel even more powerful. It is all by design.

You find yourself pitted against another love interest for mere crumbs of the Narc's attention. You do not even see it coming. That is how insane this process is. You realize that you are in the middle of a love triangle, and, instead of being angry with your Narc, you actually find yourself working harder to keep them satisfied. This is part of the Narc's sorcery. Its mesmerizing and downright wicked. You continue to lose your identity and self-respect trying to win a game in which there is no prize. You may even recognize what's happening to you, but you don't care. You are too far in. You are determined to save your marriage, family, and way of life. You want your Narc back. You crave the love bombing. You need to have it again at all costs.

What makes it even more fun for the Narc is all of the rich content they are getting from you in the midst of your confusion. When you get upset, try to find out what's going on, or chase after them, the Narc is showing off to their new love interest how desperate you are. The new love interest tries harder to win them over, and all the while the Narc is sharing their innermost feelings with them about how trapped they feel with you. The new love interest has hope. Maybe they will leave you. The Narc makes you sound pathetic. You have no idea that they speak so ill of you. They have convinced the world that they are *your* victim. People on the outside not only condone, but praise, their distasteful and disloyal behavior. For the time being, the Narc is on the top of the world.

Narcs like to keep their exes close like trophies. They are also very useful in keeping the other people in their lives on their toes. The Narc does not enjoy their own conflict as much as they love watching others go to war over them. They incite some argument and then sit back and watch. They keep their hands clean and passively watch others argue about them. It's invigorating and reminds them how sought after they are.

Triangulation is a common game played by the Narc. This is where other people are thrown into the scene of the play directed by the Narc and their sole purpose is to make you insecure and jealous. Maybe it is their ex or an attractive friend. This person is brought into the mix so that you will doubt yourself. It is someone intentionally designed to be in competition with you. Whoever it is that resurfaces, it is someone held in high esteem by the Narc. You start to question whether you are still the Narc's number one. Are you being replaced? Is this person a threat? You can't lose the best thing that's ever happened to you. The more secure you seem, the harder the Narc will try to give you reason to worry. They will intentionally dote on this person or spend a little too much time with them. They may even compare you to them. You will then work harder competing for the Narc's attention. Often times, the Narc has both parties vying for their attention. You worry that if you are anything less than perfect, the Narc will move onto one of their many other adoring groupies.

Normal human beings are able to care for more than one person at a time. Narcs only have so much emotional energy to expend on others, so the more they give to one person, the less they give to another. By holding someone else in their life in high esteem, the Narc is implicitly devaluing you. You know that your position in their story is being threatened. You are being written out of the script.

To add to your insecurity, the more significant the role that other person begins to take in the Narc's life, the more the Narc talks down to you. Not overtly, but there is condescension. You sense a disdain. Not all the time; every relationship has ups and downs. You sweep it under the rug. You may even convince yourself it's normal. After all, relationships go through ups and downs. You convince yourself that the Narc is being less kind towards you because they are growing more comfortable in the relationship. They are simply expressing themselves in a more raw and unfiltered way. However, the fights continue to hit new and deeper lows.

You let them get away with it because it's not always bad. Just like they feed you a mix of affection and rejection, the Narc praises you and then insults you. You go from being a perfect soulmate who can do no wrong, to someone who can do nothing right. You could bake them a cake, and they would comment it's not as good as the last one you made. You could write them a sonnet, and they would comment on your odd use of grammar. You could give them a present, and they would mention a gift someone else gave them a while back that topped this one. Before you know it, every little thing you do is wrong. According to them, you are incompetent and crazy.

You doubt your own abilities, recollections, and judgment, thereby becoming ever more dependent on the Narc. You need their affirmation for even the smallest of decisions. No matter how confident you once were, you are now crippled with anxiety and self-doubt. The Narc will begin to tell you what you should feel and when. They will shame you for feeling the wrong emotion at the wrong time. If you challenge them, they will make you seem overly dramatic, too sensitive, and unhinged.

During the devaluation stage the Narc acts in the most unscrupulous ways. If not openly, then in a way that makes their behavior sound justified. The lying that occurs is pathological. Because you have just come off of love bombing, you are very confused. *Which of these two people is real? My significant other can't really feel this way. They argue with me, then they treat me well. They give me compliments, but lace them with insults.*

The Narc purposefully manufactures confusion by having you experience two strikingly different realities simultaneously. This is a form of cruelty and torture that, after a prolonged period of time, will cause you to not trust your own mind. This also makes the other gaslighting they subject you to so much more effective. This inability to reconcile what is happening to you because of the seemingly conflicting actions is referred to as "cognitive dissonance."

You begin to justify the Narc's awful transgressions as being situation specific. They cannot possibly be a bad person. After all, they were so good to you for so long. They must just be going through a rough time. Any loving human being gives a break to those they care about when going through a difficulty. The Narc knows that, so they continue to feed into this victim-like role they have created for themselves to keep you being accommodating. You are so confused. Nothing makes sense anymore. You hope this stage is over soon and that things go back to the way they were. Sadly, it never gets better. It actually continues to get much worse.

The Narc goes from wanting to spend every waking moment with you, to accusing you of failing to give them any space. They intentionally create situations to make you feel rejected. For example, they plan activities for the two of you and then blame you for participating. They may even deny ever inviting you. Then they start to go out and do more things alone. They'll go dark for a period of time. You are dying to call, text, show up, anything, just to find out what happened. Why are you no longer included? Why are they ignoring you? Did you do something? It eats away at you. You go crazy trying to figure out what went wrong.

Eventually, you aren't able to take it anymore. You ask where they went and who they were with. The Narc set you up to ask these very questions. It was by design: a setup conjured to make you seem demanding, obsessed, and needy. Why would you possibly believe that you have a right to know where they are and who they are with at all times?

They feign being disgusted by your controlling nature as an excuse of why they need to have even more space from you. They pretend to be suffocated by constantly tending to your overbearing needs.

You are afraid to ask them about what they are doing when they are not with you. The more fearful you are to ask, the more they test the boundaries. They may text you and tell you they are on their way home, then not show up for hours. They may invite you to meet them somewhere, show up late, and act as though nothing happened. They may not answer their phone for a prolonged period of time. It becomes very clear that they are annoyed by you; they behave as though you are oppressing them.

To add to the confusion, all the while the Narc is very complimentary of you in front of others, making you feel appreciated and respected, so you start to forgive the nasty way they treat you in private. But while you reassure yourself that you are in a healthy relationship, they continue to demean you in private. They degrade you, trying to provoke a reaction—then use that reaction against you. You learn that expressing any displeasure at their abuse only makes you look like a crazy person. You continue to avoid it at all costs.

At this point in the relationship, you probably have lost most of the identity that you had before you met them. No matter how strong of a person you were, you are now a more listless version of your former self, due to the abuse that you have endured. When you try to make small attempts to regain your independence or do something where you want the Narc to support you, they are nowhere to be found. They do not support you, nor do they ever defend you. The

Narc wants to see you fail. They have worked so hard to isolate you from your family, friends, and former self.

You feel very alone. It's as though you are nothing more than an extra in the Narc's life—and one that constantly gets in the way. You keep trying to appease them and to add value to their life, only to be shot down. You can never satiate a Narc, because they are always moving the goalpost. The moment you think you know what they like and how to make them happy, it all changes. They want to see you try but remind you that you will never be enough. It makes them feel powerful, and it makes you try harder.

They want to see you fail because they feel inadequate themselves. While they try so hard to be perfect and to conform to what the world expects them to be, they can never quite get it right. It's a bizarre dichotomy. The Narc perceives themselves to be better than everyone around them, but still insufficient. No matter how hard they try to fit the mold, it just never feels natural. This inability to be who they are pretending to be makes them perpetually angry and always on edge. They lash out and cause scenes in private. For example, if something trivial does not go their way, they may punch a wall, throw a temper tantrum, or retreat. This reaction is due to their loss of control. When they feel low, they need to exert control over you. They get recharged by manipulating your emotions during their fits. Their tantrums usually have nothing to do with you, but they try to convince you that you are at fault.

As time goes on, they feel more comfortable exposing their bad behavior. They have tested your boundaries. By the time they start to let their mask slip and show more of their true, nasty self, they are already quite confident that you are not going anywhere—at least, not until they are ready for you to go.

The crazy thing about the devaluation stage is that you do not even realize it is happening to you. Sure, they have changed. They are crabby. They are not as kind. Yet you excuse it. You think it is just a phase. *No marriage is perfect.* That is how insidious and deep this abuse runs. You defend your abuser. It happens so slowly you have no idea what is coming next. That is what make the final blow so painful. You think it could never, ever happen to you. You are so used to the ups and downs, that you think this is just another fight. You have been through it so many times that you can't imagine they will actually ever leave you; but they do. They don't just leave you once. They leave you and return, just to do it all over again. It's nothing more than a sick game to them.

Were there signs that the person you fell in love with was evil? Sure. You realized their loyalty swayed with the wind. Whatever the Narc did to their ex, that is precisely what they will do to you. They called them crazy. Abandoned them. Met you before they totally got out of the last relationship. Wash. Rinse. Repeat. Narcs are not original. Their entire lives are a cycle of the exact same story replaying itself out with new actors. It proves that everyone is replaceable, except for them. They get a kick out of that.

The reason that the Narc picked you is because you are unique and beautiful: inside and out. What is bizarre about Narcs is that they are drawn to that which they lack, envy, and therefore eventually despise. They love people who exude warmth and joy because they are cold and lifeless themselves. They love to leech off those who are giving, because they only know how to take. They are drawn to those who love with all of their heart and soul, because they can't feel anything at all. Nothing gets them off like taking down a successful, beautiful, and independent person and turning them into someone dependent on their validation, accepting any and every kind of mental abuse fathomable.

The Narc targets people who are kind and exploits what they consider to be weakness. Their predatory nature perversely tries to lure the victim using their own compassion against them as a weapon. If the Narc starts to feel that they are losing control, they feign some sort of event that left them wounded. They either stretch the truth, or even flat out lie if necessary. Do not be surprised if they pull out all of the stops—even fake an illness if it suits them. A predator knows that by appearing weak, they can gain strength.

Devaluation is the longest phase in the relationship. This is usually because it is where the Narc gets most of their jollies. They are the malevolent director. They lie repeatedly. When you catch them, you say they did it to protect you, but that's not true either. They lie to keep you in line. This is the part in the relationship where you lose yourself. You doubt your abilities and start to question your worth. You center your entire life around catering to their whims, and you somehow convince yourself that you enjoy it, but that you are not good enough.

A common misconception is that Narcs are incapable of long-term relationships. That is far from true. They will stay in a relationship for as long as they feel in control. Often they overlap many relationships over each other. They do not owe anyone their loyalty. As long as the victim stands by the Narc's side, irrespective of their behavior, the Narc has no reason to leave. It is fun to see just how much they can get away with.

Narcs can stay married to a spouse for decades. They feel the need to live lives that conform with societal expectations. Divorce does not fit into their image of being highly sought after. They would much rather be unfaithful to their spouse than acknowledge they were involved in any sort of failed relationship.

Many Narcs obsess about looking perfect, because on the inside they experience chaos. They need the trophy spouse, country club membership, fancy cars, and accouterments to convince the world, and to convince themselves, that they are adequate. They mimic what they believe society values. The Narc doesn't stay married for love; they stay married for appearances.

During the course of the marriage, the Narc will go back and forth devaluing and love bombing their spouse. This purgatory stage of the relationship is awful, but not as awful as what is coming next. Eventually the Narc will engage in episodic discards.

Discard is a deeper and darker version of devaluation. During devaluation the Narc may pull a few disappearing acts, but during discard they are essentially "breaking up" with you. It doesn't mean they will divorce you or never see you again. It just means that they are letting you know with certainty, and in a bold way, that they have checked out of the relationship, and that you should be worried. It's a form of fearmongering designed to keep you at bay.

CHAPTER 5

Discard

This is the Narc's most maniacal stage of all: the discard. Suddenly and seemingly out of nowhere, the Narc will decide that they are done with you. You don't know whether it is for a little while or for good. No matter how permanent they intend for it to be, the Narc's way of going about it will always be the same. It will be at the worst possible time, and you will never see it coming. It will not be based in any sort of external reality, so you will not be able to predict it. Nor can you make any sense of it. The discard will occur when the Narc is feeling low about themselves and when they have someone else providing them with supply on the sidelines.

You need to understand that this event is not happenstance or a misunderstanding. Because you are abandoned without explanation, your mind tries to fill in the gaps. The Narc intentionally inflicts this cruelty on you. While it may be extreme, it is often passive-aggressive. Maybe the Narc disappears without explanation. They are much too smart to appear the villain. They even convince themselves that you deserve it. You have betrayed them in some unforgivable way, so they are justified in leaving you and causing you pain.

In their minds they will rationalize it. Maybe you have not been giving them as much attention as you were. Perhaps you questioned them when you should have blindly taken their abuse. The Narc no longer sees you as a devoted spouse, but as someone who has betrayed them in some unforgivable way. Therefore, they feel warranted in betraying you and cutting you out of their life.

Reality doesn't exist outside the Narc's mind, so whatever story they conjure, no matter how delusional it is, they believe it. This is for their own self-preservation. Even though they are well-aware they are hurting you, they convince themselves that you deserve it. All of the good things you have done, and sacrifices you have made, suddenly amount to nothing. They treat you no differently than a stranger.

Remember that people do not randomly leave those they love; people only casually leave those who they are exploiting, when they no longer serve a purpose. The Narc leaves you when they are feeling out of control and perceive that your attention has shifted away from them. Often this corresponds to a time when something awful is going on in your life, which is causing you to not be able to put them front and center. They then have the added bonus of devastating you when you are down and out. Other times the discard comes when you are focusing your attention on something else, such as your career or your children. Taking care of anything other than the Narc is a direct affront to them, for which you must be punished.

Most of the time these discards are episodic. They take a break from you. You wonder if the relationship is really over or whether they will return. Because a Narc keeps ex-lovers like trophies, they will never get rid of you for good.

The relationship will only terminate when you decide to no longer accept the abuse. The irony is that you spend so much time fearing losing them, but your fear is unwarranted. They will perpetually return. *That* is what you should really be worried about.

They will discard you for hours, days, weeks, months, and sometimes even years, and then waltz back in as if nothing ever happened at all. They condition you to accept it during the devaluation stage by getting you used to the silent treatment and little ghosting episodes. When they physically disappear during discard, you are used to this feeling of being left without an explanation. Abandonment can even feel peaceful for a bit. You can finally let your guard down. You vacillate between missing them and feeling relieved.

At times you will be tempted to make contact. They gleefully wait for you to come crawling back. There is nothing that delights them more than when you come back seeking answers, begging to know what went wrong. Reaching out is the worst thing you could do. The Narc considers you making contact as weakness and doubles down their stronghold over you.

If you go after them, they will either continue to ghost you and test how much they can get away with, or gaslight you some more. They know how badly you want an explanation. This is the perfect opportunity for them to shift the blame and convince you that you are the cause of the chaos. Chaos that you can't quite understand because it is completely contrived in the Narc's mind. You are searching for some external validation to explain why your partner is emotionally, and sometimes also physically, absent.

You are left in a fog. You have no idea what happened to you or if they are really gone. Was this just a trivial disagreement, or are they leaving you forever? You don't know if it was your fault. You are just lost, devastated, and bewildered. Meanwhile, the Narc will be carrying on with their life just like normal. They continue to engage in their activities seemingly unphased. Going about their daily lives and routines as if nothing has happened.

You are utterly and profusely broken, sulking in the darkest place you have ever been. While it seems complicated, the explanation is simple: The Narc was never emotionally attached to you. Not one bit. They do not feel anything at all when separating from you, no matter how long you have been together. They do not cherish the memories. Nor do they appreciate you. Companionship is not what makes them feel alive; it's knowing that they control you. They don't need to physically be near you in order to control your emotions. They have become masters at manipulation from afar. They know it kills you to feel as though you don't matter or even exist.

Another reason the Narc goes on without skipping a beat in the other facets of their life when separating from you is that they need to keep up appearances. The Narc cares much more about what they look like to the world than about how much they hurt their family. If they maintain their normal way of life, and you are completely distraught, they gain an upper hand in the narrative. They use your emotions against you. They may use this as proof to show others that you were a difficult and hysterical person. Any signs you exhibit of distress will be used against you as evidence of your inability to keep it together. They are quite compelling when telling their side of the story. Many listeners take the bait, believing you to be the villain.

The Narc's charming and charismatic disposition makes them a social chameleon. They can adapt instantly to appease their audience. They are experts in knowing what others want and need. Because their personalities are not authentic, they can transform on a whim. They are masters of mimicry and manipulation. While it is unbearable to accept, their relationship with you was not real. Nothing about them is real. They played the role they knew you wanted them to play. It was all a performance. That is why they can discard you without any hesitation or emotion. If they convinced you of their sincerity, imagine what they can convince others of, those who know them far less.

The Narc's uncanny ability to fool their audience is fueled by their need to win. They can fake tears, love, and empathy. They do not feel any guilt or remorse for causing pain, but they do get some jolly out of it. During the love bombing, they were empowered by knowing that they could make you feel elated. During the devaluation, they were empowered by knowing that they could move the needle of your emotions. During the discard, they were empowered by knowing that they could traumatize you.

They need to destroy you for one simple reason: They hate you. They hate you for all of the good qualities that you have. They hate you for your ability to feel, care, and love. You painfully remind them that they are incapable of these things, and you appear to mock them when you display healthy and normal human emotions.

The most emotion you will see from a Narc following a discard is an evil smirk. They generally display a shallow affect, lacking the normal emotional ranges of a human being. Sure, they may throw temper tantrums, but generally speaking they are deficient in emotional reactions because they are only replicating the behaviors that others expect them to have. You may start to notice a delayed reaction to emotionally stimulating scenarios or inappropriate reactions to mundane happenings. When it comes to the relationships close to them, their emotional range as the relationship progresses will be somewhat lifeless, yet at a public event they will display gregarious reactions, feigning depth. That is because they need to keep up public experiences.

By the time the Narc discards you, they consider you to be a burden. It's incomprehensible to you, because you are their biggest fan. You run circles trying to keep them appeased. Even though you essentially live to serve the Narc, they will get the notion that you are not sufficiently playing the role they have carved out for you. They twist things in their minds so that they consider themselves to be the victim.

They believe you took advantage of them. Therefore, they hate you and feel no sympathy towards you whatsoever. For example, many Narcs are high-wage earners and desire to have their spouse take care of the home and/or the children. This is a particularly satisfying arrangement for them, because controlling the purse strings helps them ensure you don't have the financial resources to later escape their abuse. They may pay the bills and keep you in the dark about your assets and debts. You can live in a nice home, maybe even drive a nice car, but you won't have much say over any of it. The Narc financially runs the household, but later resents that they have to take care of you. If you display any signs of independence or resistance to their demands, they consider you to be their enemy.

To a Narc, things are black or white. You are with them, or you are against them. They know best. If you question them in any way, it is an attack, and you are now the enemy. You became a different character altogether in their screenplay, and the old you ceases to exist. They do not even remember any of the good times, nor do they cherish the memories.

No matter how firmly you stand by their side and buy into their designs, it will never be good enough. Eventually the Narc will grow weary and discard you anyway. The entire discard was intentional and by design. It was no accident. Nothing could have changed it. Your relationship was destined on this path from the moment they began grooming you. It is not a matter of if, but when and how many discards you will allow to occur. They do this to destabilize you and ironically to keep you running back to them, which makes them feel powerful.

Your instinct has probably been alerting you that something is wrong for quite a while. Even during the best of times in your marriage, deep down you knew something was not right. Maybe you could not sleep? Maybe your heart raced for no reason? Maybe you had an uneasy feeling in the pit of your stomach? Whatever it was, you knew something was wrong for a long time, but you suppressed it. You had made a commitment to this person. You wanted to make it work. You tried to do the right thing, even when it felt like you should throw in the towel. You were the only one fighting. You were fighting yourself and aiding your attacker, but you didn't even know it.

No matter how evolved we believe we are, our bodies are primal. They sense danger. When your body starts sending you messages... *listen*. There is a threat. The call is coming from inside the house.

The flight or fight response in our brain is controlled by the amygdala. When you are in a relationship with a Narc, your amygdala is in overdrive. This can often be confused for passion, excitement, and lust. It's not. It's danger. The continual overstimulation of the amygdala will lead to you living in a perpetual state of fear with symptoms similar to those who suffer from PTSD. Even long after you escape, you may continue to experience residual panic attacks and generalized anxiety.

When you are left discarded, scared, and alone you naturally start to wonder: How could I have prevented this? There is nothing you could have ever done about the outcome. It was all preordained. The whole relationship was a setup designed to suit only their needs. It was plotted out from the first time the Narc laid eyes on you. No matter what you did, and how perfect you were, this is how the relationship was destined to end. An unexplainable discard as you stand by and watch them give someone else the affection that they took away from you for no reason at all.

They rarely leave for good. They know it's much more painful if you have a front-row seat to their newfound happiness. Plus, it keeps their new love interest on their toes.

For amusement, they will eventually reinstate contact. Give you glimmers of hope. They'll test just how far they can push. It's all a trap to get you to react so that they can show off to their new love interest how crazy you are and how desired they continue to be. The new love interest fears that if they step out of line, they will be discarded like you were.

You would think that when the Narc finally reinstates contact with you, that they would feel compelled to provide you with an explanation, but they don't. You likely have been conditioned to be fearful of questioning the Narc, so you may not even ask any questions. You may be too afraid to mess it up. They are back. Just leave well enough alone. All the while, the Narc loves knowing that you are dying to figure out what happened. What caused the fallout? Where did they go? Is your relationship over? This is when many people start learning about NPD. They are alone and in the dark desperately seeking answers that they can't get from the Narc themselves.

You start reading about it on the Internet. You talk to a trusted friend. You start to figure out that your spouse is a Narc. You are left dumbfounded and confused, trying to understand what happened to you. The only thing that makes any sense at all are the tidbits of information you piecemeal together in your research about who Narcs are and what they do. The puzzle pieces begin to fit in place. Reading about NPD can become addicting, because it's one of the few ways that you can actually heal. Finally, you are getting the answers you so desperately craved. It may not be the answers you want, but by comprehending who the Narc is and what they do, you can finally find your way out of the fog. When you feel out of control, you immerse yourself in your studies. This is how you take back control and find the strength to finally move on. You now know that your only option is to let the Narc go, even if it's the last thing that you want to do.

The difficult part is that the gaslighting likely still has a residual hold on you. You doubt yourself constantly. You question whether your mind is faulty. Whether you are the one with a problem. You may even question whether you, yourself, are a Narc, too. You go back and forth wondering whether NPD is even a real thing? Was your ex a Narc?

They fit the framework, but Narcs are so dark and sadistic. At one point, your ex seemed like the beacon of morality. You wouldn't have been attracted to a monster. Would you?

The confusion is crippling. The person you see the Narc as today seems nothing like the person you first met. Not even remotely. That's because the Narc's professed social mores and ethical values are purely situational. They change with the wind, depending on who they are with and what they need to accomplish. Once the Narc is ready to discard you, they can drop the mask of the morality that they took on in order to appease you.

The Narc is not grounded in a sense of right or wrong. Right or wrong depends on what suits them in the moment. This is why so many of them live double lives, lie compulsively, and appear to be so perfect to the outside world. They are often successful because they will resort to any means necessary to accomplish any end they desire. Most of their goals are shallow. That is why they build up a seemingly beautiful house of cards to the outside world that eventually crumbles from within.

While beautiful on the outside, they are depraved on the inside. They hate themselves and therefore are incapable of loving anyone else, whether it is their spouse or even their own children. Their worth comes from their control over others and their possessions. This is why going through a separation from them is particularly awful. Divorce is a direct affront to their dominance, and you are now trying to take away their things. They will do anything to ensure that you do not succeed. What you need to survive and what you contributed to the marriage is completely irrelevant to them. In their minds, you deserve nothing.

It is hard to believe that someone can be this rotten. Especially someone you once loved and probably someone who you still love. Good people want to see the goodness in others. Be careful, though. It is that very philosophy that Narcs depend on to crawl back into your life and take advantage of you once more.

Even knowing all this, some people choose to do whatever it takes to get the Narc back after the discard. If they succeed at getting the Narc back, this will only amount to greater pain and a more extreme discard in the near future. Whatever you do, be strong: Do not allow them back in.

Once they know you will return for more punishment, they will exploit this power to unchartered new depths. Each subsequent discard becomes progressively more brutal and seemingly more permanent. They test how far they can push you until you break. The harshness will escalate, and the discard will likely become increasingly public with time as it is designed to humiliate you.

The Narc is always looking for the next thrill. Eventually breaking you down and building you back up grows tiring to them, so they up the ante for a new thrill. In extreme cases, the Narc moves on and starts a whole new family, all while remaining married to you. It is astounding the things that they feel entitled to do.

The Narc doesn't believe in having a soulmate; rather, they have several trophies they bring out depending on the audience. You may be lucky enough to serve as one of the many or even rank at first place for a few years or even a few decades. Nevertheless, when it suits their fancy, they will discard you yet again.

That heinous person you saw rear their ugly head at the end of the relationship, that wasn't just a mood. That was who they always were all along. They only pretended to be someone else for a short while to pull you in. The person you loved was a demon in disguise.

The reason this all hurts so very much is not because you realize that you have lost the Narc; it is because you realize that you were losing who you were when you were with them. You miss how alive and high you felt when things were good. You know that part of your life is over. Nothing is left but a shell of memories. You are haunted by the fantasy. Your entire life while with them was built around a false premise.

Once the Narc knows that you are on to them, watch out. They will do anything to discredit you. You pose a threat to their entire existence and the lies they have told their entire lives. You have the power to expose who they are behind the mask, and therefore you need to be annihilated at all costs. It all boils down to this: If they cannot control you, they must destroy you. By emotionally breaking you down, they know that you will not dare challenge them.

Discard is one of the deepest, darkest experiences a person will ever face. It is even more cruel and lonely than experiencing a death. With death, there is closure. With a discard, the other person goes on to flaunt their life, which used to be your former life, before your eyes and make you believe that you are the cause of your own demise.

A Narc is not satisfied with terminating a relationship; they want to do it in the cruelest way possible and murder your spirit in the process. With a death, everyone comes together to comfort you. With a narcissistic discard, you are left alone, looking like the crazy one. There is nothing more sadistic than the Narc's intentional attempt to break you for nothing more than the sport and thrill of it.

As you mourn the loss of your partner and your former life, you need to be prepared for what is coming next. The Narc will not leave well enough alone. If they sense that you have moved on, they will come back. Not because they miss you, but because they want to have the pleasure of trying to break you once more.

CHAPTER 6

Hoovering

After the discard, the Narc goes missing in action for some period of time. They test you to see how long it will take for you to come crawling back to them. If you don't beg for their mercy and return, they will incidentally reemerge on their own. They find some premise to communicate with you in order to weasel their way back into your life. They genuinely believe that if you engage with them, you won't be able to resist their magnetic charm. The more you resist, the harder they work to get you back. You want to believe that they genuinely miss you and are remorseful for their actions, but the truth is that for the Narc it is never about love; it is always about control. Their attempts to get you back are referred to as "hoovering." This term is coined after the vacuum cleaner brand, because the Narc sucks you back in to treat you like dirt.

They begin love bombing you all over again. There will be an obscene number of attempts to draw you in. They will fly a carrier pigeon to the ends of the earth. They will flood you with sweet memories. Every song on the radio reminds them of you. They will say or promise anything to pull you in. This is where most victims give in to their Narc and fall right back into their scheme.

Hoovering comes in many forms. While the most common is love bombing, sometimes they will try gaslighting first. If they believe that they can get away with it, that is. They may reenter your life and pretend as though nothing happened at all. Perhaps they send you a good morning text with a sunshine emoji and no explanation. They may literally show up at your door, walk right back into your home, even if they have been gone for months, and pick up right where they left off pre-discard. They pretend life is completely normal and act as if they never abandoned you at all. They are so used to gaslighting you, that they will not think much of it. They count on the fact that you will wish the breakup never happened, so you both slip comfortably into your old roles without even acknowledging what occurred. You remain silent in fear of jeopardizing their return, and the Narc gleefully gets away with their abuse without having to give an explanation. This is the Narc's favorite outcome. They love knowing they can keep you living in a state of denial out of fear. It's the ultimate sadistic control.

Other times, they may begin by sending benign messages feigning feeling sentimental about past memories. Saying they thought of you and can't get you out of their heads. It's true: They can't. They need you to give them attention stat. They will say and do whatever is necessary to lure you back so that they can get their fix. A Narc cannot fathom the idea of you rejecting them. They believe they are entitled to decide when to turn the relationship on and off, not you.

One of the most common gaslighting tactics when hoovering is pretending to be the victim. You abandoned them. They didn't leave you. What are you talking about? You must have misunderstood the whole thing. You wanted time apart, not them. They left unwillingly. This whole ordeal was created by you. They never wanted to be apart. It's all a big misunderstanding. They continue to rely on deflection and deception to deny any wrongdoing on their part. This is a little more work for the Narc, but they still enjoy getting you to fall for their petty little lies.

If the Narc realizes that you are onto them, and they cannot get away with their fabrications, as a last resort they will fake being remorseful for everything they have done to you. The excuses will pour out of them. They had a midlife crisis. They felt hurt. They were upset by other things that had nothing to do with you. They are profoundly broken. Some may even go so far as to say they need to get professional help. They wish they could take it back. They had a breakdown. It was a brief lapse of judgment on their part. You won't believe it, but you will want to. They do not say this because they know they have a problem. The Narc is painfully aware of all their faults, but they do not view them as such. You could read them the clinical definition of NPD and they would consider those characteristics to be strengths. The only reason they offer to seek therapy is to appear weak and remorseful so you that will draw back near.

If a Narc ends up at a therapist's office, you can bet that they will try to win over the therapist. They know all the right things to say in order to appear as though they are self-aware, cognizant of their shortcomings, and desperately trying to work on making themselves better. The Narc is an actor at their core, so they know how to play the role of a good patient. It won't be long until they will spin their tale of woe so that it appears as though you drove them to their destructive behavior. You find yourself playing defense, rather than making any meaningful progress in your relationship.

If all these tricks fail, they retreat back into the abyss, wait a bit, and then soon reemerge. They convince themselves that it's a timing issue. They still have it. They think you will eventually see the error of your ways if they catch you at a more vulnerable time. They know when you are most receptive to their abuse. Often, they will reappear on a special occasion (your birthday, an anniversary, etc.). They are hoping to catch you at a time when you may be nostalgic. They will use the opportunity to make you feel sentimental and waltz their way back in. A special occasion is also a perfect excuse to love bomb you again. The Narc's vicious cycle can begin anew.

The Narc will use your kids, family, friends, or anyone else around you as a pretense to make periodic contact. They may feign an interest in or care about a mutual person or a pet in order to draw you in to a conversation that you cannot refuse. If you share children, they will suddenly take interest in the kids' activities. If they have contact with your family, they will insert themselves into those family members' lives. They believe if you will just talk to them, they will be able to drag you back in.

If the Narc fails in all these attempts, they will hoover by proxy. They will send in one of their flying monkeys to do the job. The term "flying monkeys" comes from *The Wizard of Oz*, when the wicked witch sent her flying monkeys to destroy Dorothy and Toto, all while keeping her hands clean. Don't be surprised if one of the Narc's loyal comrades reaches out to you, begging you to give the Narc one more chance. Telling you how much the Narc misses you and is hysterical without you. They will guilt you into giving them another opportunity.

The Narc uses this henchman to validate their narrative and do their bidding. This third party also advances the Narc's mission to gaslight you. They will repeat the Narc's tale of woe and attempt to convince you that you have the whole situation wrong. The flying monkey may be someone who has the very best intentions, but because they are doing the work of the Narc, their point of view has been colored with falsehoods. If you decline to return to the Narc, they will mistakenly believe you to be cruel or unreasonable. No matter how tempting it may be, be careful what you say to the flying monkey. Their loyalty is likely to the Narc. Anything you say will be shared with the Narc.

If you don't give into the flying monkey's requests, the Narc may again find a way to "accidently" run into you or even pretend that you mistakenly called them and that they are returning your call. The Narc may stalk you, which you may confuse for love. That is because in the beginning of the relationship they successfully convinced you that their random presence was an exciting and pleasant surprise. If it worked before, it could work for them again.

As an extreme measure and last resort, the Narc turns to sympathy. They either feign an illness or insinuate that they will hurt themselves. The Narc can't stand to lose, neither the battle nor the war. They will pretend to be despondent without you. The flowers have had no color since you've been gone. Life has no meaning without you in it, and that they simply won't be able to go on. If you won't talk to them directly, they'll write you. It's a great way for them to control the story. Now they don't have to contend with answering your questions or accounting for their inconsistencies. They get to tell the story as it is in their own head. To them, it's reality. No reality exists outside themselves. The message they send you will have the emotional range and depth of a Sylvia Plath novel. It will be beautiful and tragic. A dark and disturbing tale of woe written in the form of a love letter. You will cry. You will be confused. You will be tempted to go back.

These lines they feed you aren't real. They are carefully crafted to get you to engage. They know you are a good person. They appeal to your empathy, which they consider to be a weakness. If you reject them at this point, they are justified in demonizing you. They make you seem like the cold and callous one. You broke up the marriage. You destroyed the family.

When you don't fall for their games, watch how quickly they go from pretending to adore you to being angry with you again. They can no longer keep the mask up for very long. How dare you not pine after them. They find it downright offensive that you don't do as they say.

If you cave and let the Narc back into your heart or home, it will not be as it was before. There is no happily ever after. Rather, they will punish you dearly for your disobedience. There is no repairing a relationship with someone who is so damaged. Just wait until they start testing you again. It won't be long. If you thought it was bad before, you haven't seen anything yet. The Narc came back for nothing more than sport to humiliate you, degrade you, and teach you a lesson.

You so desperately want to believe that the Narc has changed. The entire thing was a bad dream. You misunderstood. You blew things out of proportion. You overreacted. The person you once knew is still there. They love you. It was just a hiccup. Most people go through the cycle of breaking up and rekindling the relationship with their Narc a countless number of times until they finally recognize what is happening to them.

The loop of love bombing, devaluation, discard, and hoovering continues until it exhausts itself and something breaks. Some people cannot let go of the Narc because they never feel as though it is really over. The Narc has come in and out of their lives, physically and emotionally, so many times that this revolving door begins to feel par for the course.

While it is usually a blessing to save a marriage, trying to repair things with a Narc is dangerous beyond measure. They are only trying to pull you back in to break you. If you give them enough chances, they will succeed.

They don't want you back to love you. They want you back to control you. They can't handle rejection. They are going to bring you back in so that they control the narrative of your breakup, only now in a much darker and more humiliating way. They will use the opportunity to ensure that you become increasingly dependent upon them. They will force you to cut off your ties with those that genuinely care about you by making you select your loyalties.

They demand you prove your love—even though they are the one who left—by constantly forcing you to put them first. The people closest to you, those in whom you confided during your times of crises, will in turn also feel betrayed. You can't win. The Narc will do anything and everything in their power to make sure that the next time they decide to discard you, your support structures will be weaker than ever.

Sadly, most people fall for the bait: hook, line, and sinker. They know exactly what the Narc is trying to do but fall for it anyways. It is easy to go back to the past. It is the path of least resistance. Your mind wants to believe that if something served you well once before, it can do so again. It is difficult to reconcile that something that was once so wonderful can now be so harmful. This cognitive dissonance is complicated by the gaslighting.

It's tempting to want to believe the Narc and all of their pretty little lies when they try to come back. You desperately crave answers. You pray that it was really all a giant misunderstanding. However, if you truly want to comprehend narcissism, read the rest of this book, scour the Internet, and talk to a mental health professional. Do not ask for an explanation from the Narc themselves. You will never get an honest answer from a sociopath.

You can get so caught up in what you want that you forget what you deserve. If you think the change of moving forward is hard, you can't imagine the pain of staying where you are. One day you will wake up and be grateful that you decided not to settle and that you took your power back.

I wish I could tell you that the Narc will make a single hoovering attempt, and if they do not succeed, that they will slip away quietly into the night—but they won't. In fact, they will try to win you back harder every time you reject them.

Narcs cannot accept defeat, and they actually enjoy a challenge. They are so used to easily getting their way when manipulating people, that they consider it a personal challenge, and an even greater victory, when winning you over is difficult. You must resist them no matter how tempting it may be to reconcile. The only way to beat the Narc is to stop feeding them with any supply.

Remind yourself of how the Narc acted when you were melancholy. Did they care about you, or did they proverbially kick you when you were down? While in life we are typically told to focus on the good, when dealing with a hoovering Narc, you need to focus on the bad. Remind yourself of all the horrific and inhumane things that they did to you. Remember how they made you feel on your darkest days.

If you reconcile, it will not be long until the Narc reverts back their former repulsive ways. You will end up disgusted that they pulled the wool over your eyes yet again. The idea of getting revenge on such an evil person sounds so appealing. You find some comfort in the idea that that there is some ultimate cosmic retribution and accountability for one's actions. You want to know that they can't just get away with it time and time again.

If you really want to hurt the Narc, live as though they did not exist. Ignore them. Prove they are insignificant. Attention, good or bad, breathes life into them. Ignoring them is the most excruciating death. You need to play their own game against them.

Do you remember how cruel it was when you were the recipient of the silent treatment? Return the favor. Show them they are unworthy of explanation. Don't give them the opportunity to converse with you or creatively excuse their transgressions. Stay strong. They initially did it to you because they know the silent treatment hurts. It hurts them even more, because they are so desperately craving constant attention and control. If they cannot communicate with you, they cannot influence you. By not giving them a speaking part in the film that is your life, you take away their power. They feel helpless. This is how you succeed.

No matter the form of the hoovering, cut them off immediately. You should be offended they continue to attempt to torment you for their selfish gain. Narcs hoover because they are feeling low on supply. They need to feed their fragile egos, and who better to do so than someone they already know how to play.

Turn the tables on them. Don't fall for the sweet and empty nothings they try to whisper in your ear. Play on their insecurities and reject them. Going back is much too dangerous. It's not even an option.

CHAPTER 7

How to Leave the Narc

You may be wondering: How can I leave the Narc if they have already discarded me? Well, discard is never permanent. The Narc abandons you. Then they hoover. Your relationship has plateaued, so don't expect the initial love bombing phase to return in all its glory. Rather, there will be many cheap replicas of it that follow. The Narc goes through some of the motions, but you are no longer worth the same amount of effort to them. They are an expert on reading you at this point. They know exactly how much work, attention, and affection they need to expend in order to get you to stay, and they will not give you an ounce more than is absolutely necessary.

If you want to turn the tables on the Narc and have the upper hand, you shut the door to the relationship after they discard you. You leave for good. You pack up your things. You don't provide an explanation. You certainly don't provide a warning. You don't reason with them. You just go. Separate yourself from them both physically and emotionally.

I realize that it's not that simple. Sure, there is the emotional part, but how about the practical parts? What about the entanglement of your finances? What if you are in the same home? What if you share children? What about your mutual friends? You can't just pick up and leave your life. Well, to some extent you may just have to.

Before taking any decisive actions, be sure to consult with a family law attorney in your area. They can advise you as to how best to break away and preserve any legal claims you have moving forward. You can bet that when you are dealing with a Narc, things are going to get ugly. You need to stop looking at this person as your spouse. You are no longer in safe territory. You need to plan your escape. How do you situate yourself so that you walk away with the most that you can to rebuild your life? How do you protect yourself? What will you do next?

If you want to salvage any bit of the life that you currently have, you need to leave and start over. This is somewhat ironic. There is a cost to leaving, but the cost of staying is often much higher. If you stick around, you may very well lose everything that you have. Take what you can. Ensure your children are safe. Make sure that you are financially independent. Then cut the cord and get as far away as possible given the constraints of your personal situation.

By the time the Narc discards you in the relationship, there is nothing left worth holding onto. Perhaps there is a crumb of attention and affection if you comply with their demands for public admiration, but there is nothing left of substance. No love. No emotion. No caring. In fact, they despise you.

When you are at the point where you know that you need to terminate the relationship, you need to be committed to your course of action. You need to cut all ties with them to the extent that you can. Anything that you and the Narc still share together can be a tool and gimmick the Narc uses to at first innocuously communicate with you and then later manipulate you. They will perpetually punish you for rejecting them.

By accepting their discard, you are essentially calling their bluff. They tried to play you, and they got one-upped. You beat them to the punch. They believe they are the only ones who can decide when it's over: not you. When you make any moves to end the relationship, they start to question themselves. They wonder if they are losing their touch. They miscalculated. You outsmarted them. And most importantly: You saw through their mask. They know that you are aware of just how evil they really are. This terrifies them. They fear exposure and the lack of control over your story.

Once you are at the point where you are done, do not ever let them back into your heart. If you do, they will make you pay for what you did. They will show you who is boss. That is why maintaining no contact is critical. Notice this chapter is not called, "How to Get Over the Narc." That is dealt with later. Your safety comes first. You need to detach yourself before you can start to heal.

No matter how amazing you were to them, no matter how great the relationship was, they will never miss you. They are not capable of it. You might miss them, but don't you dare show it. They are like sharks who smell blood. Any inkling that you miss them, and they will manipulate you so badly, you won't know what happened.

Besides, you don't actually miss the Narc. You miss how they made you feel. You miss the rollercoaster. You miss winning them over. You miss the love bombing that would follow. The Narc just misses controlling you.

If you start to doubt whether this was all a misunderstanding and wonder whether they really do care about you, just remember this: A Narc is absolutely aware of what they are doing. Think about it. Why do they act one way in public and another way when they are alone with you? Have you ever watched the Narc switch roles in an instant? Boom—just like that. They turn off who they were with you in a particular moment and act completely different in front of someone else, without hesitation. Normal people can't turn emotions on and off like that. Only actors can. They are constantly playing a role that changes the script to appeal to whatever audience is in front of them at the time. They are 100 percent aware of their words and actions and have complete control over them. When they treat you poorly, it is intentional.

As tempting as it may be when you part ways, do not reminisce. Your mind will try to go back to the love bombing stage. It wants to stay there. Snap out of it. Rather, you should think of all the terrible things they did to you. Reread this book and remind yourself that you were a victim to a setup. Remember that there is no possible way for you to have a happy ending with the Narc. You need to maintain a realistic perspective of your relationship and remember that this person has little positive attributes to offer you in the future. It's bizarre, because even though you know in your heart that you need to distance yourself, you will struggle staying away. Especially when they hoover. You need to remain strong.

I'm not going to lie to you: It hurts. It hurts like hell. And just when you think that you are finally over them, you'll be faced with another reminder of how things used to be. You will be confronted with another memory, and it will all come crashing back, like a rip current pulling you into the sea. You feel hopeless when you let your mind rest. For a while, you simply must not let yourself go there. A healthy amount of denial and detachment are necessary to recuperate. Do not let your mind wander back to the good old days, because it is more dangerous than you will ever know. If you become sentimental, you will doubt yourself, and then you are at risk of returning to a toxic situation.

At times you will wonder what life would have been like if you were still together. Do they miss you? What are they doing now? Let me spare you the pain. You could not have been together, because it was destined to end from the day it began. They do not miss you. Right now, they are love bombing someone else and likely visiting the same places they used to go to with you.

Maybe you are lucky enough to have a few trusted friends and family members around who can help you objectively discern what happened to you. People who will believe you when you tell them about how the Narc behaves when no one else is around. People who have the common sense and life experience to identify the Narc as being a negative presence in your life. You need a support system that is going to help you make a clean break. It is critical to have people who you can call when you are feeling weak and tempted to go back to your abuser.

No matter how many times the Narc discarded you, no matter how permanent the break seems, the Narc will always come back for another round to ensure they still have control. It may be a while, but eventually they will resurface when the opportunity strikes. Narcs feed off of knowing they still have you no matter what. Even if it is just watching your eyes well up with tears. They thrive off of being able to affect your emotions.

How do you make the Narc leave you alone for good? A well-known technique is referred to as the "grey rock method." You want to become as imperceptible and uninteresting as a grey rock. Blend in. Aim to be dull. Don't react to their provocations. Like a bully on the playground, the Narc only taunts you while you respond to them. If you are unphased, you are no longer entertaining. They will eventually wander off and go manipulate someone else. Narcs are addicted to drama, but since they always want to appear innocent, they rely on provoking you rather than overtly causing a scene for which they could be considered responsible. If you ignore them, they can't play. There is no point in convincing the Narc they are wrong or explaining to them how much they have hurt you. The Narc won't receive the message. The only thing they will hear is that they are still getting under your skin. Knowing that they cause you misery breathes life into them. Do not give them the satisfaction of knowing that they are the source of your pain.

The grey rock method means that you also superficially suppress yourself in their presence. Typically, in a breakup scenario, you want your ex to see how good you look and make them regret leaving you. That is the last thing you want to do with a Narc. They are drawn to a shiny, pretty object. You can easily lure them back in. You don't want to. Don't show them how happy, beautiful, and successful you are. They will accept the challenge to bring you down. Show them nothing.

You are better off wearing a boring outfit and pretending that your life is entirely uninteresting when you know you will run into them. If they think that they have used up the best parts of you, they may move on to their next plaything. While normally we want our exes to wish they could have us back, with a Narc you should pray that they find you dull and repulsive. Hope that they meet someone else and move on.

The grey rock method is much easier said than done. The Narc is not just some random person in your life; they usually have been, or may still be, the center of your world. How can you not react when they have stolen everything from you? How can you not want to make them regret what they have done? No matter how tempting it is, and irrespective of how much they hurt you, ignore them. It is bad enough that they took your past; do not let them have your future.

Resisting the urge to tell them how you feel will be painfully difficult. In the beginning you are only be pretending to be numb. Inside you may be flooded with a range of emotions. It can feel as though you have been punched in the gut when you hear the sound of their voice. Your instinct will tell you to respond, but your brain will tell you to stay quiet. With time you gather the strength to be a silent observer. The quicker you learn to contain your emotions, the less control the Narc will have over you. There is a certain empowerment in being able to sit back, observe, and not participate in the folly. Only then can you start to see the Narc's petty games for what they are.

That does not mean you should fail to stand up for yourself or be fearful to speak to them; rather, it means that you don't feel compelled to convince them of anything.

You get to a place where you don't care what they think or what they do. There will undoubtedly be instances when you will need to speak with them directly, such as when you are dividing assets or dealing with children, but when you do, respond in a diplomatic and businesslike manner. Speak from your head and not your heart.

This breakup is going to be so much harder than any other you have ever experienced. The Narc's games created a deep emotional bond and psychological dependency. In other relationships, you work through the realization that you are losing a companion. In this type of relationship, you start to realize that you actually lost yourself. You feel lost, shattered, and alone.

It's not until you let go that you realize there was nothing worth holding on to. Even during your closest times with the Narc, they were completely emotionally unavailable. They feigned caring about you until it no longer suited them to do so. The truth is that you had been alone the entire relationship. However, actually *being* alone would have felt a lot less lonely.

In normal relationships, there's a chance that people can grow and evolve. Things can get better. Both parties can sincerely try to make the relationship work. It is never like that when one of the parties is a Narc. If you reconcile, you will experience a very brief love bombing, which is hardly even remnants of that which you so long for from the beginning of your relationship. Then it will be immediately followed by punishing you for daring to try to run away or to expose their NPD. You will be in a hell deeper and darker than you ever imagined possible. This is why you have to unequivocally understand that making up and trying again is not an option—no matter how desperately you want it. If a Narc crushed you once, they will absolutely do it to you again. You can guarantee that it will be even more insidious the next time around. Get out as quickly as you possibly can.

Once you successfully walk away, and the Narc realizes there is no hope of tangling you back into their web, they turn diabolical. The Narc is usually in denial that you will ever leave. It's not until they find themselves in divorce court that they realize you are serious about not taking them back. It's then that the gloves will come off and you see more clearly than ever who they have been all along.

CHAPTER 8

Preparing for Divorce

You are here: Whether by your own volition or necessity, you and the Narc are legally parting ways. In order to outsmart the Narc in the courtroom, it is necessary for you to dissect the destructive rollercoaster ride you have been on. Divorce starts in your mind long before it can proceed in the courtroom. Prior to engaging in any legal battle, you need to study your spouse. Irrespective of how long the two of you have been together, this person is now like a stranger. The person you once thought you knew doesn't exist.

Too many people want the shorthand of how to overpower the Narc in the courtroom, without fully taking the time to grasp how Narcs operate in life, love, and war. You cannot beat your opponent until you really know them. That is why so much of this book is devoted to exposing the Narc's tricks and explaining the darker side of your relationship. Once you understand their modus operandi, you can use their own poison against them. None of this will be easy, but the price of peace will be well worth the cost.

Divorce is one of the most traumatic things that a person can endure. Divorcing a Narc compounds the challenges one would ordinarily have to face under the circumstances. This other person has been slowly eating away at you for so long, that you do not even remember who you used to be. By the time that you figure out your spouse is a Narc, you have likely been drained of your resources, depleted of your emotional strength, and are weighed down by fear. You have probably lost a great deal of your self-confidence and have become dependent on them both financially and emotionally. Unfortunately, that is precisely the time you need to be the strongest of all.

When you come to the realization that divorce is inevitable, you must move swiftly. This is very difficult to do, because you are simultaneously grieving the death of your marriage. To cope with that loss alone is challenging enough. At the same time, you are forced to prepare for what will be one of the most difficult battles of your life. The person who was supposed to protect you is now your opponent. In the midst of your sorrow, you need to be smart and spring into action without delay. The Narc has been putting themselves first since the day you met. You have a little catching up to do.

The Narc likely was able to willingly get you to hand over your financial independence by selling you on a dream: the fantasy that you could have everything you ever wanted so long as you let them be in charge. It would be their pleasure to take care of you. Stay home. Quit your job. Do not further pursue your education. Do not worry about dealing with the bills. They gave you permission to live a life of leisure. Or so it seemed. Who wouldn't be sold on that dream? It's like winning the lottery. Your soulmate promises to take care of you. The price to be paid, unbeknownst to you at the time, is total submission to their every whim.

The promise was empty. No matter how much money you had, your life was never a cakewalk with them. Maybe you had nice things, but you worked for them harder than anyone. You slaved away, catering to all of their needs. They piled responsibilities on you, and you no longer had a meaningful say over who you were or what you wanted to do. There was never any gratitude in return for all your efforts. The promise of freedom was actually total bondage.

By the time the two of you are parting ways, you have been awakened to the harsh reality that the Narc intentionally tried to strip you of who you used to be. You find yourself in an inferior earning position. Your once-upward trajectory is a fleeting memory. You used to be so independent and driven. What happened? You used to be in control of things. When did that change? Now you don't even know what financial accounts you and the Narc share. If you do have access to the accounts, it's likely only to the ones they want you to have. They gave you the perception that your lives together were an open book, but there is so much you didn't know. You are slowly starting to discover that the person you were married to had countless secrets. They didn't begin misbehaving when the marriage was rocky; they had been keeping secrets from you from the very beginning.

By keeping you in the dark, it was easy for the Narc to hide and dissipate assets without your knowledge. During the marriage, it was sport. After you part ways, they want to ensure there is as little left as possible to be divided in the marital estate. Even if you lived a comfortable life with all the material things you could desire, somehow when you are disclosing assets in the divorce, the Narc confesses that you are both paupers. They want you to come to the conclusion that you can't afford to get divorced so that you will stay in a bad marriage—and they will have more control than ever before. Many Narcs fake being broke when it suits them. (Then again, other Narcs fake being rich.)

Sometimes the Narc's preoccupation with appearances means that there really are few assets of value. The mansion is underwater. The cars are leased. There are loans on the retirement accounts. The credit cards are maxed out. Money is owed to the government for back taxes. The student loans have yet to be paid. On the outside, you appeared to have it all. Unfortunately, the material things were just an illusion of success. The Narc leaves a mirage wherever they go. Even if they managed the household finances, they blame you as the reason you are both now destitute. They allege that you were fiscally irresponsible or failed to contribute.

In addition to the Narc having a stronghold over the financial estate, they also have an advantage when it comes to the psychological trauma that accompanies a divorce. They never were emotionally vested in you. The reason they can carry on as normal and go about their daily lives after the two of you part ways, is because they were never attached to you in the first place. While decent people grieve the loss of a spouse, no matter how good or bad they were, the Narc is not dealing with that sense of loss. The only thing that they care about is themselves, and the only emotional turmoil they likely are feeling is a sense of rage, that you feel entitled to "their" hard-earned money and things. To the Narc, this is war. You need to commit yourself to a course of action to ensure that you are ready to face the battles that lie ahead.

The first step is putting together your support network. This includes your family and friends, mental health professional, financial advisor, divorce coach, and attorney.

Draw Your Inner Circle Close

You need a handful of trusted people who you can call on day or night, whenever you are feeling weak. The grief of divorce comes in waves. One minute you are fine. The next you are beside yourself. It's not always predictable when you will be feeling down. Who are you going to call when you need someone to pick up on the other line in the middle of the night?

These should be the people in your immediate network who you can confide in without any fear of repercussions. You can speak candidly. Admit that you miss your ex, even when it sounds silly. You can speak your truth without a filter. This should be a very, very small group. Don't tell all your friends and acquaintances your problems. Many people don't want to know, and others can very well use this confidential information against you. You need to be very careful who is privy to your most intimate thoughts.

This group should have undivided loyalty to you and to you alone. Be sure they have no allegiances with the Narc. The last thing you want is your private musings being relayed back to the Narc and used against you. The Narc will try to infiltrate your inner circle. Make sure that the people you are talking to cannot fall prey to the Narc's soliloquy.

Keep in mind that while your inner circle may make the best sounding board and provide you with strength when you need it most, they may not have specialized knowledge or intimate experience with the divorce proceedings or the psychological impact of narcissism. Therefore, their advice, no matter how poignant, does not replace that of a licensed therapist or attorney.

Very few people understand the depths of narcissistic abuse and the pain that it causes to the recipient. Often the Narc is so good at hiding their bad traits, that even when you explain what is happening, others still do not understand the magnitude of the cruelty. This can be incredibly frustrating. You feel invalidated. The most important thing is that your inner network believes you, understands you, and comforts you. They are the front lines. They don't need to be experts; they just need to love you unconditionally.

Seek Out a Mental Health Professional

Narcissistic abuse can take a serious long-term toll on your psychological well-being. It is imperative that you work to repair the damage the Narc has done. This includes facing the trauma of divorce, healing from emotional abuse, learning to trust again, finding your voice, dealing with emotional regulation, overcoming the grief, and setting boundaries. Your family and friends can help you find peace, but a mental health professional can help you take things to the next level.

NPD is particularly fascinating because the victims often find themselves in therapy more often than the person who suffers from the mental disorder. Narcs do not believe they have a problem. The problem is everyone else failing to conform to their expectations. The Narc does not have a desire to change, so therapy is of little value to them. The only time they will go to therapy is if they are using it as a tool for further manipulation.

Healthy people know that seeking help is a sign of strength and not weakness. They work on themselves and actively do what it takes to improve their overall well-being. Divorce takes a huge toll on your emotions. Have a therapist you can trust in your corner to help you cope with this major life change.

Find a Financial Advisor

It is likely that the Narc controlled the finances during the course of your marriage. They may have intentionally locked you out of accounts, failed to disclose assets and debts, and now you find yourself lacking financial literacy about your own personal situation. You may not have any clue about the scope of the marital estate, much less what you should be entitled to.

A financial advisor can help you understand your current circumstances and, in tandem with your divorce attorney, can help you prioritize what type of financial settlement you need to seek to rebuild a life for yourself. They can help you understand how certain investments work, the anticipated return, how to manage your accounts, the tax consequences, and the risk factors. Because Narcs tend to be very successful in business, many times they have complicated investment portfolios. Work with someone who can help you dissect the nuances of various holdings.

Many Narcs are high-powered executives with complicated compensation packages. Maybe they have a form of deferred compensation that you don't even know about, much less know the value of. Don't leave money on the table.

While it likely makes sense to find a financial advisor even before you enter the courtroom, this is someone who you can continue to work with long after the divorce concludes. You are looking for a professional with whom you can develop a long-term relationship. A financial advisor can help you invest and manage your settlement proceeds. The Narc is no longer your retirement plan. Find an advisor who can provide you with a sense of fiscal security at a time when things feel extremely confusing and unstable.

Invest in a Divorce Coach

A divorce coach is an integral, and often underutilized, resource. This is a professional who is an expert in the divorce process and can help you develop and implement a personalized plan to work through what is likely the most difficult and confusing time of your life. If you are struggling making decisions, feeling discouraged, angry at your spouse, and are confused by the legal system, a divorce coach is a must.

Many people decide to work with a coach prior to the legal filing of a case in court in order to determine whether divorce is even the right choice. This is especially the case when one is contemplating leaving a Narc. After years of gaslighting, Narcs can cause their victims to doubt their perceptions. A divorce coach is like the best friend that you never had. You can bounce ideas off them. They make the complicated seem simple. Your coach has an extensive amount of knowledge regarding the divorce process and ideas for how to rebuild your life thereafter. They reignite you with hope when it feels lost.

During the pendency of your case, the coach can help manage expectations, rank your priorities, and reality test hypothetical settlement outcomes. Overall, a coach works with you on a much more personal level than your attorney and can help you ensure that your time spent with your attorney is being used most effectively.

Keep in mind that your coach is not a mental health professional. They are not there to treat anxiety, depression, or abuse, but they can help you find your joy. Sometimes what a person healing from a divorce needs more than anything is hope. Maybe you have forgotten what is like to be optimistic and excited. You may have lost sight of who you want to be and what you enjoy doing.

A coach can work with you to redefine who you want to be moving forward. Post-divorce, you need to refresh your identity. Sometimes that means going back to a simpler time and looking at who you were pre-Narc. Your coach can help you undergo a makeover inside and out. All the while, they are your cheerleader and provide you with motivation when you need it most. They do this by helping you frame goals that are measurable and then making sure you remain accountable. They can also help you become a better co-parent by providing you with the tools you need to improve communication with your ex.

Meetings with your coach will focus completely and totally on you. This is a radical departure from your life with the Narc, and that is why it is so important. Often divorce is focused on the Narc and their bad behavior. Coaching brings back the focus to you. Overall, a divorce coach can be an incredibly valuable member of your recovery team.

Lawyer Up

You should retain a divorce attorney well in advance of filing any paperwork with the court. Many people make the mistake of starting to look for an attorney when they are in their lowest emotional state. They start putting together a legal team after the Narc knows that divorce is on the table and is scurrying to make plans of their own. The earlier you retain counsel, the more prepared you will be. An ounce of prevention is worth a pound of cure.

Finding the perfect divorce attorney can take some time. The more reputable the attorney, the longer it will take to find an available appointment. You may hire the first attorney you meet, or it may take a few tries to find someone who you feel is the right fit. You need to choose an attorney who you connect with and who has the requisite skill and ability to protect your interests. Choosing the right attorney is one of the most important variables that will determine your well-being during the pendency of the case and the outcome thereafter. This decision should not be taken lightly.

You may want to ask your family and friends for referrals. You should check out their online reputation and reviews. When you speak with them, find out if they have dealt with spouses who have had NPD before. Sadly, even some of the very best divorce attorneys are not equipped to negotiate against a Narc. You will find that many lawyers are outright dismissive of NPD. They consider narcissism to be a buzzword, inwardly roll their eyes, and treat your case in the same manner that they do every other in their repertoire.

You have to understand that most divorce lawyers are cynical. It is not necessarily because they are callous, but rather because they have no idea the depravity that a victim of NPD has endured. Every single client that a divorce attorney meets with claims to be a victim who was wronged and abused in some way. Some have. Some have not. Remember, even the Narc plays the victim to their own lawyer.

It is easy for your attorney to believe that it takes two to tango in a nasty case, and if you are a party, it is likely that you are just as culpable. However, cases in which one spouse is plagued with NPD is an exception to that rule. When divorcing a Narc, one crazy spouse can single-handedly cause all the chaos, at no fault of the victim.

While an attorney does not need to know how to treat this psychosis, any lawyer working in a family law context should be adept to recognize the signs of NPD and common tricks pulled by the Narc spouse. Narcs have a high rate of divorce, and domestic relations litigators will find themselves in the presence of Narcs quite frequently.

When you initially meet with potential divorce attorneys, tell them that you believe that your spouse is a Narc and see how they react. Are they dismissive? Or do they express an insight as to the unique issues that present themselves when dealing with such a damaged spouse? If your attorney is immediately dismissive of this disorder, seek different counsel. You don't have the time or money to waste in explaining it to them.

Narcs pose a different set of challenges than your typical ornery and cantankerous litigant. That is because they don't appear to be difficult. They appear to be calm, collected, and reasonable; but behind the scenes they are monsters destroying everything and everyone that crosses their path.

A Narc is not just someone who is selfish or loves the spotlight. They have a demented sense of humor. Their joy is your suffering. Someone with NPD will use any system in place to come out shining like a star and to torture whoever they feel is not holding them in the esteem that they deserve. This is what you need your attorney to understand.

Attorneys who have a strong background in NPD know that they will be able to appeal to the Narc's desire to look good and play on that. The Narc has this compelling need to seem altruistic and rational in front of everyone except you. They put on the mask and play the role of the fair, reasonable, and even-tempered spouse who is the victim of your insanity.

Too many people make the mistake of seeking an aggressive attorney. They want a pit bull to finally put the Narc in their place once and for all. That's actually the last thing you want. You need an attorney who knows how to adapt to their circumstances just as well as the Narc does. The Narc doesn't control people by acting like a jerk; they take over by being likable.

Being offensive is not the same as being aggressive. Aggressive implies unnecessary hostility. You want to keep the tensions down as much as you can while maintaining control of the situation. Your attorney needs to be slicker than the Narc. They need to know how to dominate the case without the other side even having a clue that they are calling the shots. This means filing just the right number of pleadings, keeping deadlines on a short leash, and ensuring the case is properly moving forward. Control in the courtroom is rarely achieved by the loudest voice. In fact, that's typically a sign of a weaker, less knowledgeable, and insecure lawyer. The attorney who has the upper hand is the one who is affable and carefully crafts their words. The last thing you need is one more hysterical actor stirring the pot.

If your attorney immediately plays hardball, files a slew of pleadings, is unwilling to negotiate, and lacks basic decorum, the Narc will see that as an attack and justify responding in kind. Know your enemy. Your Narc is preoccupied with seeming wholesome, good, and playing the victim. Don't give them justification to behave badly or to appear as if they are merely defending themselves.

On the flip side, you don't want a passive attorney who only plays defense and allows the Narc to run the show. Rather, it's about balance. You want someone who is not afraid to stand up to your ex but has a good disposition. They need to be well-versed in the courtroom but also understand that the courtroom is to be used as a last resort. This should be someone who able to assess the situation and respond accordingly. Ideally, they should be more charming and calculated than the Narc. It's wise to outsmart the Narc, rather than try to intimidate them. We will discuss strategies to use during litigation in the next chapter.

Escalated conflict leads to delayed settlement, higher legal fees, and handing over to attorneys the money that would otherwise be divided between you and your spouse. Many Narcs take the approach that they would rather give away all of the money to the lawyers than pay their spouse a dime. Be careful to not hire an attorney who plays into their hand.

Ensure Your Modes of Communication Are Secure

The Narc has been keeping surveillance on you since the inception of the relationship. In the beginning they disguised this as being infatuated with you. During gaslighting they convinced you that you should have no expectation of privacy and that you are entirely incapable of making good decisions for yourself. Whatever excuse they had, it was always about control.

When they feel you pulling away, they tighten the reins. This isn't because they miss you and want to feel connected. They want to make sure they don't lose their grip. They fear you catching onto them or, even worse, revealing who they are to others. They feel entitled to know everything you do and say.

You may want to consider creating a new email account, having your computer and cell phone scanned for spyware, checking your car for tracking devices, and changing all of your online passwords. They would love nothing more than to be able to log in to your bank account, calendar, or email. Knowledge is power. Suffocate them at the source. The Narc hates when you set boundaries.

Obtain Access to Cash

The Narc will work very hard behind the scenes to ensure that you don't have the means to pay for your basic living expenses or to obtain proper legal representation. They do this so that you either return back to them begging for mercy or are completely disadvantaged in the legal fight ahead.

If you do not have an independent source for generating income, put a plan in place for when the Narc tries to cut you off. While there are many remedies that you can pursue in the legal system with the assistance of your attorney once they are retained, ideally you should have some sort of immediate access to cash in the event the Narc pulls any dirty tricks. You don't want to find yourself in a position where you are struggling to put together a retainer to obtain counsel or your debit card getting declined at the grocery store.

You should be thinking about the following: Do you have access to marital credit cards? Do you have credit cards that they do not have control over? Did your spouse change any of the spending limits? Is your name on the bank accounts? Do you have any accounts in your sole name? Do you have cash on hand? Do you have family who can help you in a bind? Do you have any way of readily generating income should you need to be able to do so?

Gather and Save Data

Collect as much information about your finances as possible before your Narc gets wind of the idea that you want a divorce. By the time you and the Narc are knowingly about to part ways, it is likely that they have limited your independent financial resources. You may not even have passwords to the joint bank accounts or credit cards. You may not even know where your accounts are located.

Assemble as much information as you can about your financial institutions, retirement accounts, mortgages, vehicle loans, safe deposit boxes, etc. If you have any joint accounts, go to the bank and request the last several years' worth of statements. This way you know if the Narc has moved money around and you have the records before the Narc has had the opportunity to hide things from you.

It is often challenging to get a Narc to comply with discovery requests during the pendency of a divorce. They consider themselves to be above the law and know that it can often be tedious, expensive, and time-consuming before a judge slaps them on the wrist to comply. Besides, even when they must answer for their actions, they'll just lie. The Narc probably has separate accounts that you know nothing about or money that they are hiding in someone else's name. You can work with your attorney as to how to uncover hidden assets, but the more work you can do on the front-end, the better off you will be.

After you file, the Narc may deny that certain accounts exist, block your access, or move around massive sums of money. By having records of your finances, you will be much better situated to enlist the court's assistance. Your attorney can advise you based on the information you have what should be done next.

In addition to financial records, preserve any communications between the two of you. Generally speaking, it's healthy to cut the Narc out of your life as much as possible, but do not delete or destroy any records. It's common that when you are trying to get rid of the reminders of someone's toxic presence to delete, remove, and throw away anything that reminds you of them. While there is some wisdom in that concept, you should nevertheless preserve any photographs, emails, and text messages you have with the Narc. Do not look at these things and reminisce; rather, hold onto them in the event that you need to prove something later in your case. The Narc is a compulsive liar. You have no idea the things they will eventually say, do, or make an issue out of. The more evidence you have in your repository, the better.

Take a Hiatus from Social Media

In the last chapter we explored the value of going grey rock. You want to be as uninteresting to the Narc as possible. This is completely contradictory to the point of social media. We don't usually post how boring our lives are; to the contrary, we post the highlights. People post photos where they look and feel their best. Narcs love social media because they live their entire lives only showing people preselected snapshots of their reality. The Narc will follow your social media accounts, even if it means using a fake profile and alias. They may convince a friend to give them access to an account. Narcs are natural-born stalkers. They will be watching you even when you do not know it.

They will stalk your social media channels incessantly. Not because they love you or miss you, but rather because they want to know whether you are speaking about them, and they are also looking for things to use against you later. There are really no benefits to maintaining social media profiles during a divorce case. Everything you do or say will be used against you.

It can be particularly difficult to go dark on social media at a time when you are feeling vulnerable and isolated. This is usually the time when you need other people's support the most. Be that as it may, it's much too dangerous to excite the Narc and attract them back into your life, or, alternatively, provide them with valuable information to hand over to their attorney.

Determine the Right Time to File for Divorce

While Narcs sometimes file for divorce themselves, more often than not they would prefer that you initiate the legal filings. Narcs don't like the stigma of anything that is associated with failure. They look at an unsuccessful marriage as a scarlet letter, which starkly contrasts with their image of a picture-perfect life.

Besides, if you file first, they can continue to pretend that they are the victim and that you are to blame for bringing the marriage to an end. They didn't want out; you did. This is great fodder for gaslighting if you decide to later reconcile. While they are almost always the aggressor of any conflict, they never want it to appear that way. Narcs are incredibly passive-aggressive. They may corner you so that divorce is the only option you have and then blame you for making the decision. In front of family and friends, they are shocked and devastated. They hope that their message gets back to you so that you will feel guilty and ashamed.

Another reason that Narcs are less likely to file is because they do not tend to dispose of their exes. They would much prefer to string you along in the background. They don't feel the need to terminate one relationship before commencing the next. Divorce serves little purpose to them. They have no desire to divide assets or pay you support. They would much prefer living a double life and using your marriage as an excuse as to why they cannot commit to their next partner. It keeps that other person on their toes. The Narc is subliminally telling their new love interest, "Don't misbehave, or I'll go back to my spouse." It's just another form of triangulation.

Unless the Narc has a compelling reason to file, they will avoid it for as long as they can. They count on the fact that you won't have the courage to proceed. They may even provide you with just enough financial support so that divorce may seem not to be in your best interest. Maybe they move out but continue to pay for the house. Perhaps they pay your credit cards, but the limits are barely enough for you to survive. It's because of tricks like these that you should meet with a divorce attorney as soon as possible.

Every situation is unique. Based on your individual circumstances, it may or may not make sense to file at that given moment. You need to be able to make an informed decision on how to best proceed. Every gift they give comes with a price.

In all likelihood, the Narc has already spoken with an attorney. They always plot ahead. Even if they have not formally retained counsel, they likely have discussed the prospect of divorce with an informal acquaintance or friend. They are being coached. Life is a chessboard, and they are always thinking about their next move.

Even if filing for divorce from your Narc is an unequivocally good idea, there may be timing issues that should be taken into consideration. You should always seek the advice of a licensed divorce attorney in your state to understand how the particular laws of your jurisdiction should impact your decision. Things to discuss with your attorney include: What will happen to the house? Am I eligible for support? Does the length of the marriage matter? What will the custody battle potentially look like? Divorce is not one-size-fits-all.

After you retain an attorney, and know in your heart that divorce from the Narc is the only option, you may have to be the one to pull the trigger. It is so difficult to be the one accountable for ending the marriage, but you should know that the marriage ended long before anyone ever met with a lawyer. You need to have the strength to believe that you are worth more and that you can and *will* do better.

CHAPTER 9

Divorcing the Narc

Despite the adversarial nature of the legal system, there are never any real winners in divorce. You can certainly have a strategic advantage over your opponent and take actions that will positively impact the overall outcome in your case, but divorce is shrouded in so much loss. It's a brutal process, where a family is torn apart and the household's financial resources are divided between the parties and their lawyers. Most of the time neither spouse is able to maintain the lifestyle to which they were formally accustomed.

Even though divorce comes with a heavy price, if you are married to a Narc, you know that the value of peace is priceless. You may have no other option. While it all seems fatalistic, there is a light at the end of the tunnel. While divorce itself is horrific, it is a temporary state. Transforming yourself afterward can be quite beautiful. Before you can get there, though, you need to deal with the practical challenges that lie in front of you.

Here are some ways that you can gain leverage and maintain an upper hand in the midst of a contentious divorce proceeding against the Narc.

Do Not Reveal Your Emotions

As a general principle, the person who keeps their composure during a conflict is the one in control. If you can maintain discipline over your own emotions, you can maintain control over the situation. Narcs don't feel great joy or sadness. The emotion they are most comfortable in is rage. A rage they have learned to control their entire lives in order to play a certain role that suits them. The Narc has mastered internalizing their anger and appearing above the fray on the outside. They turn emotion on and off as it suits them, not when they are authentically experiencing it. While this is an unfortunate way to go through life, it's a great way to handle negotiations. Wearing your emotions on your sleeve will cost you. A poker face wins the hand.

If you are confronted with the Narc baiting you during your case, no matter how strong you are, at some point you will react, whether it is with tears or anger. It takes great strength to not emote in any way in their presence. The Narc methodically chips away at your sanity and self-control. They do so in a way that is very private. It's insidiously passive-aggressive. Most people on the outside will not even recognize the viciousness. You may not even realize it is going on. Narcs are so smart, but they always use their power for evil. To the outside world, they are placid while portraying you to be manic. If they ever do let their crazy show, clearly you were the cause.

When you must communicate with the Narc in the presence of the lawyers, you will be infuriated by the audacious and blatant lies they tell. You will be tempted to unleash all of your pent-up anger and expose them for the fraud they really are. Resist the urge. You can and should set the record straight, but one of the biggest mistakes you can make is losing your temper. Remain calm and collected. They are trying very hard to get under your skin. You want people to listen to your words, not your tone.

During your relationship with the Narc, somehow, they convinced you that you were not allowed to be angry or point out any of their wrongs. They either made you feel that you had no right to do so, or you were simply terrified of the response. You became accustomed to bottling up your feelings. No matter how rotten the relationship became, you pent it all up inside. The level of the abuse ran so deep that they took away your permission to feel.

Once you realize what the Narc was doing to you, you cannot unsee it. You will be furious that they are continuing to try to get away with their tricks. There is so much you want to say. You want to call them out on all of their inconsistencies and half-truths.

After some time away from the Narc, all of these caged-up feelings may pour out of you. You start to realize how badly they emotionally abused you. You are bursting with frustration. This delayed realization amplifies the intensity of your feelings. The amount of time it takes for each person to experience this varies, but when it does finally occur, you will be outraged. Whatever you do, do not cave in to the temptation to release your emotions now. Do not lose your composure now or make a display while in litigation. Not only will you make irrational decisions, but you will appear to be the crazy one. The Narc is desperately trying to deflect and make it look as though you are the one who is cruel and out of control.

When they witness you having an emotional outburst, they take the credit for being the catalyst. It empowers them. They are not saddened or hurt by anything you have to say, but rather vindicated. They will use your reaction as an example to their new love interest, attorney, and the court as evidence of how crazy you are. The longer you keep it together, the harder they will try to break you. They will begin to act out and resort to more desperate measures, and inadvertently their mask will fall and their true self will show. Your goal is to get them to snap first. The way you do it is by not engaging in their attempts to lure you into the fight. Let them keep getting bolder until their lunacy reveals itself.

One of the Narc's greatest talents is pushing your emotional buttons. Your failure to emote will, in turn, make them blow a gasket. That's exactly what you want to happen. Do not express any emotion. Do not insult them. Don't reminisce. And whatever you do, do not get angry. (Not in front of them, anyway.) Your failure to react to them means that they are losing control. You throw them off their game and make them doubt themselves.

Since the day they met you, the Narc has been methodically memorizing your every move. Their precision in the execution of causing you pain is unmistakably intentional. The Narc has been paying very close attention and testing out what things hurt you to the core. They want you to feel the same pain they feel. It invigorates them to know that you are in distress and that they are the cause. It empowers them with a sense of godliness. They cannot control their own emotions, so they vicariously take hold of yours.

The monster you see in divorce court has been there all along. They act no worse, but it will certainly feel that way. The Narc had you under their spell for so long you did not even realize the extent of gaslighting. You thought that you and your Narc were playing as a team, but all the while they saw you as an opponent. Divorce exposes the underlying game of war that has been happening beneath the surface all along. The most vicious contempt and hostility is reserved for those closest to the Narc. The Narc will say and do the cruelest things imaginable to those they are supposed to care for.

The Narc is hoping that by saying the most spiteful things to you, usually in private, that you will react publicly. You will lash out. You will look like the aggressor, and they will appear to be the victim. The Narc gets great delight from showing their friends, family, and attorney how you have become unglued. Sure, they may have been attacking you behind closed doors for years, but the moment you defend yourself, they will be sure that it will go viral and be taken out of context. They will intentionally provoke you with the most hurtful words possible. Going straight for the jugular, they will take whatever you hold most dear, or are most sensitive about, and use it to their advantage. They will go after your greatest love or greatest fear, because in their minds they should hold the most sacred place in your heart—even after they have discarded you. Even if they do not care one bit for you, they expect to be forever worshipped and feared. Indifference towards them is a direct assault. Keep in mind though, indifference is your only option.

Whatever you do: Stay calm and play it cool. Do not take the bait. The less you react, the more they will. Some people mistakenly think that if the Narc understands how much they are hurting, they will begin to let off. It's just the opposite. The Narc gets off on inflicting additional pain when you are down. Do not appeal to the heart; they don't have one.

If you want to kill the Narc, ignore them. They cannot take it. They need your attention, good or bad. You need to look at divorce court as a business. Put your feelings aside for a little while, because you need to focus your energy on prevailing in the litigation. That is not to say the emotional stuff is unimportant. In fact, it is the most important thing of all; but divorce is not going to provide you with emotional fulfillment or retribution. Healing happens outside of the courtroom. Your settlement is going to give you the tools and resources you are going to need during the recovery phase so that you can move on with the next stage of your life. The healing almost never happens simultaneously with the divorce. Let your attorney fight your legal battle, while you focus your efforts on finding your former self.

Negotiate through a Third Party

I typically advise my clients to take whatever steps necessary to work things out amongst themselves, seeking the involvement of outside powers only as necessary. Internally crafted solutions are usually more satisfactory to the parties and reduce the costs of a divorce case. Divorces with Narcs are very different. The imbalance in power dynamics makes it nearly impossible to negotiate without a third-party observer. Remember, the Narc is preoccupied with how good they appear, not how good they truly are. They tend to be kinder in the presence of an audience. However, sometimes that in and of itself will not be sufficient to cure the imbalance of power. Once the Narc feels comfortable, they will start to work the room. They will turn on their charm to try to convince the mediator that you are irrational. They will again try to bait you to fall prey to their digs.

Much like you must act like a grey rock towards the Narc when they attempt to hoover, you need to resist the urge to respond to them in the way that they deserve. Remain calm, no matter how hard they work to get under your skin.

You also want to have as little direct contact with the Narc as possible during the pendency of the legal proceedings. In most situations it is not wise to engage in direct negotiations with them at all. You are probably better off to fight from a distance. The Narc knows your weaknesses all too well and will exploit them at any given opportunity. Throw them off their game by cutting off their oxygen. They are used to manipulating you. Give them someone else who is an unknown variable to contend with, rather than you.

This is a far cry from your typical divorce case, where it is ideal that the parties have ample and open communication, limit the attorneys' roles, and work together towards an amicable resolution. When one party is a Narc, you want to limit private settlement discussions. Pretty much any communication with a Narc will be turned against you. They may offer you the false hope of reconciliation so that you will go easy on them or so they can gather information from you. Just like when they love bombed you to find out your desires and tell you everything that you always wanted to hear, they will do the same at this stage. The Narc will give you whatever you need in the moment to make you believe they had a lapse in judgment and to draw you back in or to give them something they do not otherwise deserve.

They have been pulling you in and pushing you back for so long, that sometimes they just do it for sport. In the process, they acquire more information to behave in a maniacal manner against you when the opportunity strikes. These people are dangerous. You must keep your distance and hide your hopes and fears in front of them for self-preservation. Resist the temptation to open up to them. They want to know what is most important to you so that they can go after it.

Focus on Relevant Legal Arguments

All too often victims of NPD become obsessed with the idea of proving that their spouse is a Narc. This is an exercise in futility. It is likely is not worth your time or resources trying to expose the Narc, because even if you succeed, it very well may not impact the outcome of your case. Many victims mistakenly believe that the courts will see through the Narc's bad behavior and compensate them for their abuse. That is simply not true. While divorce law in the United States is state-specific and every situation is unique, as a general principle you will not be compensated for your spouse having less than admirable character. Talk to your attorney about whether there is any value in having your spouse undergo psychological testing, and whether the results could meaningfully help your case.

Emotional abuse is something that is unfortunately all too real, but almost impossible to prove. The Judge will generally not give you a greater share of the marital estate or more spousal support because you were married to a jerk. Spending any energy trying to convince the court that you were dealing with a Narc is likely a complete and total waste of your effort. This is a devastating realization.

Do not have the false impression that the courts will give you the vindication you crave. You are sadly only a number in a cruel and overloaded system. Do not mistake the court system for a platform to expose the Narc for who they are.

It is often far more important that your attorney knows that you are both up against the Narc, rather than the court. Work on having your attorney assist you with attaining the best settlement possible under the law so that you can go on to build a new and better life. You have spent enough of your energy focusing on them.

That is not to say that the dark behavior that your ex exhibits is completely irrelevant. For example, if the Narc's behavior is damaging your children's mental, physical, or moral well-being, that specific behavior may need to be addressed so the Judge can take necessary action to protect your children. If your spouse engaged in an affair, you may have a right to seek compensation for the money they spent on their paramour. The point is that you should focus more on exposing the Narc's behavior and how it is tied to a pertinent issue that remains to be decided in your case, rather than the idea of exposing them as a Narc. Not everyone will understand what that label means, and an overburdened legal system with overworked participants is not likely going to learn through your case.

This is where you will need to work closely with your attorney to narrow down the issues, understand how they apply your state's law, and then parse out what facts are relevant to your legal narrative. Many people make the mistake of telling their attorneys every nasty thing their ex has ever done, which can be very costly, and may or may not be of consequence in the divorce proceedings. It's tempting to want to tell them everything. You are trying to paint a simple picture of a very complex situation. Give your attorney an outline of the facts and then ask them where you should go in-depth. Understandably this is easier said than done, because so much of the Narc's abuse is not direct and straightforward. The cruelest things they do require a lot of buildup and explanation, because they intentionally engage in behavior that cannot easily be proven or witnessed by the objective observer. Nevertheless, you are likely paying your attorney by the minute. You want to be selective about how you use your time, both one-on-one with your lawyer and also with what arguments they make in the courtroom. Your attorney will help you understand which facts and arguments are relevant based on the specific laws of your state. Stay on track. Remember: The goal is to walk away with the most possible in the divorce. This is far more important than proving your spouse is a schmuck.

Remember They No Longer Control You

When you are in a relationship with a Narc, you are their willing prisoner. Once the relationship is over, the cognitive dissonance makes it hard for you to escape your former dynamic. You may have been conditioned to succumb to the Narc's needs. This notion cannot be erased overnight, and the Narc will try with all their might to keep you trapped in this mindset.

The Narc is an insecure and frightened bully. They depended on you to keep them feeling alive, and then they grew to resent you merely because they needed you. Does it get any more psychologically twisted? They hate you because they find themselves dependent on you. They were trying to make you dependent on them, and they feel as though you tricked them and turned the tables. You tried to pull a fast one. Because they look at emotional entanglement as weakness, the closer to you they get, the angrier they become. The Narc has an oxymoronic view of you as their source but also as their nemesis. That is why as the relationship progresses, they become more hateful toward you.

As time went on, you became accustomed to feeling unsafe and not wanting to trigger the Narc's evil episodes. This trepidation of walking on eggshells is hard to shake. The Narc relies on the aftershocks of their abuse, betting that you will not rock the boat during litigation. After all, they are in charge. You would not dare defy them in any way.

It is important that you understand that unlike any other relationship you have experienced during your life, where shared experiences bond people together, to the Narc, the day you no longer serve a purpose, you mean nothing to them. They do not see you as a person who has good and bad traits or someone with who they once shared a future. Things to the Narc are black or white. People are good or evil. After discard, you are enemy number one, who must be destroyed at all costs.

While you may be thinking, *This is someone I once loved*, they are ruthlessly contemplating your demise. There are a few reasons for this. First, they blame you for ruining their happily ever after. Whatever false vision they held for the future, you have now made impossible. Secondly, you know them for who they really are. Their whole life is based on a lie. You know the truth. If you expose them, they are done for. You pose a serious threat. Third, everything in their life comes down to control. They feel that they have lost control of you, which makes them feel as though they are losing control of themselves.

No matter how much they stifled you during the relationship, you now need to find your voice. The Narc will try to manipulate and intimidate you into giving in to their demands. Do not feel pressured to do as they say in order to keep them appeased. You should know by now that the Narc is never satisfied. The more you give, the more they take.

Appeal to the Narc's Vanity

In order to prevail, you will need to play upon one of the Narc's biggest weaknesses: their constant and ever-present need to look good to the outside world. You already know them for who they are, but they can still fool everyone else in your case. They are driven to appear fair and generous. The Narc will go to great lengths to hide how self-interested they are. Work it to your advantage.

A good attorney knows that a successful settlement involves creatively framing the issues. For example, your spouse may be completely opposed to paying you child support, but they are terrified of being labeled as a "deadbeat parent." They want to pretend there are no assets to divide, but they cannot stand the thought of being labeled a failure. They don't believe you deserve a single thing, but they will avoid seeming unreasonable.

The only way to get anywhere with the Narc is to understand it is all about them. They need to look good at all costs. You can use this to your advantage. It's easy to want to threaten your ex, but you can accomplish a lot more by playing nice and cornering them. They will never openly choose greed. They try so hard to appear fair and reasonable. Put them on the spot, and they will very often do the right thing, but only because they are terrified to look evil.

Look for Hidden Assets

The Narc is a compulsive liar living a double, or sometimes even triple, life. They have no conscience. They have fantasized about leaving you since the day they met you. It was never about building a life together; it was about making sure they had everything they wanted and could keep you dependent upon them.

Sure, they will pretend that everything belongs to both of you, because that is what they are supposed to say, but in reality they believe they deserve everything and that you should be destitute. They subscribe to the mindset that, "What is yours is mine and what is mine is mine."

You can bet that they have been hiding things since the inception of the relationship. If they have a safety deposit box that you know about, you can almost be certain that there is another that you know nothing about. One is for show, and one contains the good stuff. Extreme Narcs can hide things as egregious as another significant other. The world is their playground. They believe they are entitled to do whatever it is they want with whomever they want. No matter what it is, you can bet that they are hiding things. The Narc will never let you really know them. It would make them much too vulnerable. By the time you are in divorce court, no matter how many things they kept a secret from you, they are kicking themselves for telling you as much as they did. The Narc always has and always will look out for themselves first. This means that no one can be privy to their secrets.

Talk to your attorney about whether it is worth issuing discovery in your particular circumstances, and if so, to what extent. Discovery is the formal request for information.

It can be from the spouse directly or from another third-party entity. Discovery can be one of the costliest parts of a divorce case, but, depending on the circumstances, it may be well worth it. This is another area where it is very important to have a strong rapport with your counsel. Many victims of NPD feel as though they have been so blindsided by the entire relationship that they are desperately looking for answers. It can be tempting to spend valuable resources seeking an explanation as to why the Narc discarded you, why they are so damaged, etc. That is not the purpose of discovery. Those are not the answers you will receive. The purpose is for you to obtain a greater share of the marital estate, receive a greater amount of support, and/or be awarded more time with your children. You and your attorney need to decide whether it is likely any hidden assets or valuable information can be uncovered that will meaningfully impact your case. It comes down to a cost-benefit analysis.

Let the Narc Make the First Move Towards Settlement

No matter how fair and reasonable your settlement suggestions may be, the Narc will likely consider them to be ludicrous. They play by two sets of rules: one that applies to them and another that applies to everybody else. Regardless of what you propose, they will consider it to be unreasonable. Yet if they suggest the very same thing, suddenly it's genius. For that very reason, the Narc should be the one to make the first move of suggesting an offer.

They need to believe the idea is their own in order to stand behind it. At minimum, the idea needs to come from one of their attorneys. They will never buy into your concept, no matter how much it serves their own interest.

Their pride will not allow them to accept that you came up with the solution.

The challenge is that, depending on their attorney, they may not be inclined to settle. It can be very frustrating to be in a position where the other side isn't even trying to negotiate. Litigious attorneys may prefer to drag the matter out and capitalize off of your misery. At a certain point, someone is going to have to make some effort at getting the case resolved. If possible, you would prefer that it be your spouse. The last thing you want to do is sell yourself short.

The Narc Needs to Believe They Have Won

Narcs will do anything to win. Their fragile egos cannot bear the thought of anyone getting something over on them. Divorce court gives them the perfect setting to justify implementing whatever means necessary to cause you anguish after they consider you to have declared war.

Narcs get giddy at the thought of gaming the system. They enjoy learning the legal framework and then using the system to further their goals. Narcs change the rules often and unexpectedly. They will demand that you play at their pace. If the Narc has the resources, they will likely inundate you with baseless motions, making ridiculous allegations, and have you drowning in legal fees while furthering their smear campaign. They know no limits. The only thing more joyful to them than winning is watching you lose.

Here is the thing: Despite the title of this book, there are never any winners in divorce court. You end up losing a member of your family, hurting others, and giving away many of your assets to the attorneys. It is a losing proposition for both parties; but sometimes you have no choice but to play the hand that you are dealt. You win when it's all said and done by living a better life sans the Narc.

The Narc is shortsighted. They are focused on winning in the public arena of the courtroom. You win on a much bigger scale by no longer having the Narc's toxic energy drain the life out of you. You win by reclaiming your joy. You win by moving on. The Narc cannot escape themselves. No matter how many shiny toys and bobbles they may have, they can never experience any inner peace or satisfaction. They are terrified of being perceived as inferior, so in order to save face, they need to walk away the victor.

You have to craft a settlement agreement so it sounds like they are getting the best of you. It does not mean that they are. When you talk to your attorney, tell them the top three objectives in your case. Then tell them what you think that your spouse's top three objectives would be. When I say objectives, I mean tangible outcomes in the case. Too many people's expectations of the legal system can be unrealistic. By having these types of discussions with your attorney, they can help you ensure that you come away with what is most important to you, while creatively making the Narc think they are prevailing all the while.

To the Narc, it's all about perception. They are a shallow hologram lacking depth. As long as they can walk away thinking that they got one over on you, they can end the case. They will never quit if they believe that you are ahead. Because of the Narc's preoccupation with how they look, they cannot bear the thought of coming in second place. Even the idea of a fair settlement is repugnant to them.

They must come out on top in any situation. Make them believe that they have.

Whatever you do, do not be forthcoming with the Narc about what is most important to you, because that is the very thing they will go after. Turn their own game on them. Sometimes, as a negotiating tactic, it can make sense for you to feign that something is important to you that is rather insignificant. Be careful though, because this can backfire. If they easily give in, you can end up with something you do not really want. Narcs are not usually sentimental about any possessions, but they will go after anything that you hold dear. It can sometimes make sense to throw off their scent. Finally, when you let go of the thing you could care less about, they feel as though they beat you. If they can fake a relationship, you can fake their victory in a legal battle.

Do Not Let the Case Consume You

The most powerful asset you have is your mindset. The Narc controlled you during the marriage by messing with your head. They would gaslight, pick fights, and put you down. If the Narc can keep you feeling hopeless, they know you will not have the strength to fight for yourself in the divorce.

You need to remember that this state you are in is temporary. This is the hardest time of your life, but you will pull through. Don't obsess over the case like you obsessed about your Narc. It's easy to let the proceedings gnaw away at your insides. Your stomach turns just thinking of your case and all of the infinite ways it could turn out. You are completely justified in feeling anxious, but you cannot wallow in the misery of your case.

When it comes to your legal matter, there is a point where the attention you give it has a diminished return. You need to deal with deadlines and keep the matter moving forward, but ruminating over your case day and night is counterproductive. Your attorney will tell you when you need to give your case attention, and during those times you should do so. What you want to avoid is putting your life on hold for the sake of your case. Do not wait to be happy until your case concludes. Keep yourself busy. Spend time with your friends. Try to enjoy a full life outside of your legal proceedings. It is not healthy for you to remain consumed by the litigation. It will not make it go any better or faster—in fact, quite the contrary. When you cannot rationally step back and reassess your situation, you will likely make poor decisions.

Hold the Narc Accountable

The Narc is not used to answering for themselves to anyone. They tend to not be involved in things in which they cannot make up the rules. Remember, Narcs are all about control. They cannot stand the thought that they are just like everyone else and that the rules of the legal system apply to them. After all, they are always the exception.

If the Narc files frivolous motions, whether to intimidate you or bleed you dry, make sure your attorney makes them meet their burden at every turn. They may file preposterous emergency motions when they feel bored and the need to punish you. They may fail to comply with discovery requests because they consider themselves to be above the law. They may blatantly lie in writing, and even under oath, feeling invincible and laughing at putting the onus on you to discredit their narrative.

Meet fire with fire. If there are any weaknesses in their pleadings, file a motion seeking particulars to support their claims. If their outlandish allegations do not come to fruition, seek attorneys' fees and costs. Make them work for it and punish them whenever possible. The problem is, while this strategy is often necessary and effective, it is incredibly costly and not an option for the average litigant.

None of this is to say that you should be overly or unnecessarily litigious. Simply do not allow their attacks to go unchecked. If they prematurely seek the court's intervention based on lies, turn the tables. They think they can terrorize you and that you won't dare return fire. They will underestimate you since you often held back from challenging them during the relationship. Fight back and stand up for yourself with the guidance of your attorney.

Filing pleadings should not be done in a cavalier manner. This strategy, if implemented, also comes with great risk: not only the cost, but also giving the Narc an open invite to utilize the court system. You risk that your pleadings will work their way before the court, where the Narc can gain a platform for their compelling soliloquy. They love to hijack the stage and play the victim. They are charming, extroverted, and charismatic. They have absolutely no qualms lying and are very good at exploiting systems once they figure out the rules.

Most people hate divorce court. It is painful, costly, and all around unpleasant. Narcs are different; they thrive off of it. They enjoy staying connected to you even if they don't particularly like you. Litigation is an easy way to do just that.

Do not forget that while the Narc has low emotional intelligence, they are an evil genius. They are experts at testing boundaries and knowing exactly what they can get away with. They will likely lie about things that others have no way of disproving. As a bonus, their mockery of the system will get even more under your skin. If you have the right attorney, they can expose the Narc for the fraud they are. A good one can even do it with a smile.

Do Not Expect to Appeal to Common Decency

Unlike most people, Narcs do not have the ability to compromise. They never had to during the marriage. They will remain grounded in their position no matter how illogical it may seem. They are completely unwilling to accept any criticism or accountability for their own actions, so do not even think you can reason with them.

Plus, they are naturally vindictive. They get joy out of the most difficult parts of divorce cases. They want to see how far they can push you, until you break. It is a game to them and often worth the price. Since they typically leave you at the time when they feel they have limited your access to resources and stockpiled enough for themselves, they will usually be in a superior bargaining position.

Many divorces come to a settlement when one spouse waives a white flag. Perhaps they can no longer take the financial or emotional devastation. Anyone who has fought with a Narc knows all too well that the Narc loves to kick you when you are down. They have absolutely no compassion. They have no sympathy for how downtrodden and defeated you feel. Never let a Narc know you are feeling weak. They smell blood and will take advantage. A normal person would let off; a Narc sees your vulnerability as an invitation to increase their torture.

No matter how good you were to them, they hate you with every part of their being. Do not expect any kindness, or you will be hurt even more than you already are. Narcs lack all empathy but are great at pretending to be compassionate. They will lull the other actors in your case to believe they are endowed with sympathy. A Narc is a natural con artist. They are good. After all, they fooled you, and that is why you are here. Do not let them get the last laugh. Appeal to their vanity as opposed to their decency. Trying to reason with them or to convince them to do the upstanding thing is futile.

Most of us have internal limits of what is acceptable behavior. We do not intentionally want to hurt others. Even if we are angry with our Narc, we will have some self-imposed limitations as to which behaviors are appropriate and how far we'd go in harming another human being. Not Narcs. They employ a scorched-earth policy to all perceived threats. If they had a slogan in court, it would be, "Damn the torpedoes!"

End the Litigation as Soon as Possible

If possible, you want to avoid going to hearing or trial. This is true of all divorce cases, but even more important when you are married to a Narc. Narcs are great actors and can do a phenomenal job on the stand. A judge only has only a few hours, or sometimes mere minutes, to hear each of your respective stories and make a permanent decision that will have a major impact on your life.

Sometimes, though, you have no choice. The Narc wants to go to trial. This is usually for three reasons. First, they believe they can charm their way out of anything (because they usually do). Second, as an intentional strategy to deplete your resources. Narcs often have high-powered positions and are successful at what they do. They accumulate resources, but hide them well, so they can outspend you in the litigation. Lastly, it is a way to stay connected to you and continue to torture you. They are not looking to stay connected to you because they still care; rather, they are addicted to the control they once had over you and love knowing they can still crawl under your skin.

The best way to come out ahead in each and every single divorce is to get out of it as soon as you can. The more time you spend in court, the more marital resources you and your former partner are going to lose. Ultimately, whatever you end up fighting over will go to the lawyers. Most fights are not worth the money, and personal property is just about never worth the price.

Narcs who find their way into the system become addicted to the drama. They get to play victim and soak in positive reinforcement from the outside world and their next target, all while getting negative attention from you. Why would they want it to end? They get high off the attention and the conflict. A Narc thrives by making every little thing a big deal. That is because to them, it is. All your possessions and every decision that needs to be made signifies their power over you. They cannot let go of the control. Therefore, they will attempt to exert any emotional reaction out of you to continue to get their fix.

The Narc may intentionally drag out the case as a strategy on their part to financially exhaust you until you are left without legal representation. They put on a great game. You may lose your lawyer because you do not have the money to replenish the retainer or because your attorney falls for the Narc's lies, believing them to be reasonable and you to be vengeful and unrealistic. Talk to your attorney about ways to conclude your case and what a reasonable settlement looks like. The aim for any divorce is to obtain an equitable result and get out of court as soon as possible.

While the divorce process will be difficult, you will eventually come out of it and feel a sense of peace. Its normal to feel lost at first, but with time, the confusion will subside. No matter how strongly you know that leaving the Narc is the right decision, it will still hurt. Divorce is a loss, and the only people who fail to grieve are the Narcs themselves.

After the divorce process concludes and you are no longer living in the fear of uncertainly, you can start to rebuild your world. Make sure that the choices you are making during the divorce process move you towards creating the life you envision moving forward. It's easy to get stuck trying to make it day by day, coping with the emotional turmoil and legal proceedings, but you need to be looking forward. The decisions you make today should be setting you up for a better tomorrow.

If you do not share any children with the Narc, you may very well never have to speak to them again. If you share children, however, to some extent the two of you will have to remain in contact in some capacity for the rest of your lives. If that is the case, read the next chapter to know what to expect when co-parenting. If you do not share children, skip forward to the following chapter on the Narc's smear campaign.

CHAPTER 10

Co-Parenting With the Narc

Never regret having children with the Narc. While the relationship with the Narc themselves may have been very ugly, the children that resulted from your union are a beautiful gift. You cannot regret anything that brought you to this point; you just have to figure out how to move forward in the healthiest and most productive way possible.

When you share children with a Narc, completely cutting the Narc out of your life, or the children's lives, is likely not an option. While Narcs can potentially be harmful to their children's upbringing, they tend to be very good at learning all of the right lingo to dupe the court into believing that they are stellar parents who genuinely care for the children's well-being. Keep in mind that they tend to be model citizens, so they also know how to appear to be the perfect parent.

This can be infuriating to witness. The idea of the omnipresent Narc can be daunting, but it does not have to be overwhelming, Despite the obvious challenges, there are things that you can do to set boundaries and protect your children. By knowing who you are dealing with and the common tricks they pull, you can take away some of their power. By anticipating their next move, you gain control over the situation. The reason breaking up with the Narc was so hard to do is because they caught you by surprise. You were in shock when you realized you were married to a cold and heartless stranger. The Narc was able to hurt you so deeply because you had no idea who you were contending with. Now you are ready. You have gained the knowledge you need to make sure that your children are more protected now than they were before, even if you cannot be with them at every moment.

You will instinctively want to protect your children from the Narc, the same way you wanted someone to come in and protect you. You wish that you could just keep them away from the Narc, but that is likely not a choice you have unless the court determines that the Narc poses some sort of serious endangerment to the kids. Typically, there is an exceptionally high burden to meet to keep a biological parent away from their child. Narcs rarely pose an obvious threat. Their life is all about keeping up appearances. They can put on a great show.

While most Narcs behave in very similar and predictable pattern, that is not always the case with how they treat their children. Perhaps it depends on what the root cause of their narcissism is. Maybe those who have experienced childhood traumas versus those who received extreme adulation connect with their children in very different ways. They may look at childhood and the definition of parenting very differently.

Some Narcs, once they abandon the marriage, abandon their families. They can walk away from their children with no remorse. They go off to start new families and have no emotional attachment to anyone or anything. These are the vilest Narcs of all. They treat the children as collateral damage and forsake them during a discard. They may later resurface, causing just as much damage as they did when they left.

Other Narcs will pretend to be superstar parents, although they have grossly deficient parenting skills and insincere motives. They are inconsistent and unreliable. They allege that their children come first, but they only see the children as pawns in the litigation and as a tool to control the other parent. The children may never realize that their parent is playing up to them, and, frankly, it's probably better that they are unaware that they are being used. The Narc's motivations are misguided and their actions are rote. Maybe they care to the best of their capacity, but it's cold and awkward at best. They try to love, but they are incapable of it. They mimic what they see other parents do and what they pick up in films. They essentially love bomb their children, going through all the motions of being a perfect parent.

Lastly, there are Narcs that can feel love for their children, but it's conditional. They admire their children when they see their children as a reflection of themselves. A "mini me." However, this adoration only lasts so long as the child gets in line and conforms to the Narc's expectations. In this instance, the child may take on many of the Narc's less-than-flattering qualities. To gain the Narc's approval, they must become an extension of the Narc themselves.

The reality is that in a divided household, the child almost always falls from the Narc's good graces. It's impossible to keep two parents happy who have such divergent worldviews. You are teaching the child how to be loving and compassionate, while the Narc is teaching them to be cunning and manipulative. The child is in the middle, trying to meet both parents' expectations. This is an untenable and conflicting position. The child feels like they are always failing one of their parents. If the Narc senses the child has loyalties to you, they will start to pull away from the child and express their disappointment.

No matter what kind of Narc you are dealing with, there will be difficulties that lie ahead. You are raising a child with someone who lacks basic empathy. It is inevitable that you will face some trying times. Here are some of the challenges you can expect when co-parenting with a Narc.

They Will Never Put the Children First

Parents instinctively tend to do what is in their children's best interest. They look out for their well-being and make sacrifices to ensure that their children thrive. The Narc is completely incapable of putting anyone above themselves. They are not willing to make sacrifices for another person. Their most trivial needs will be prioritized over those things that are of great importance to their children. Accordingly, children of Narc parents can be very prone to disappointment and feelings that they are unworthy.

The Narc cannot even comprehend the fact that they are not making their children a priority or how their actions make them feel. The Narc cannot place themselves in anyone else's shoes. Other people's feelings and perspectives are irrelevant. They even teach their kids that emotion equals weakness.

They Will Weaponize the Children

Narcs are users. Everyone in their life serves a purpose. When they are in public with the children, they use them as a tool for attention and adulation. In private, they use them to get back at you. They know how much you love your kids, and they will always come after what you care about the most. Therefore, they will always try to turn your own children against you. They will feed them with lies. They want to convince the kids that the divorce is all your fault and that you broke up the family. Their end goal is alienation. They believe that if they can successfully pit your children against you, they will grow increasingly dependent on the Narc. Greater dependency equals greater control.

The Narc will pull many of the same tricks they use with adults on their children. It doesn't matter who is collateral damage in their wicked games. The Narc doesn't even consider it. Triangulation is normal to them. They especially love it when the children have to take a side. Unfortunately, one of the most damaging things a parent can do to a child is make them feel as though they do not have permission to freely love both of their parents.

They Will Never Be Accommodating

You can't always plan out what a child is going to do or what they are going to need as they grow older. Parents must work together to accommodate unexpected situations that arise. A parenting plan, no matter how well thought out, will always require some degree of flexibility and innovation. It is impossible for attorneys to draft a rigid agreement that will seamlessly apply to each and every possible contingency situation and continue to make sense for years to come. Parents need to necessarily make judgment calls and work with one another outside the scope of any written legal agreements.

You will never get that level of cooperation from a Narc. They are completely inflexible. They will hold you to the terms of your written parenting plan that is entered with the court, even if they never abide by it at all. Per usual, the Narc will continue to test the limits. Do not expect them to cut you a break or to do you a favor. They will refer to the rules when it suits them and ignore them when they don't. Irrespective of what they do, the Narc will expect you to religiously conform to the parenting plan, even when it doesn't make any practical sense given the situation. The hypocrisy is astounding.

They Will Trash Your Parenting Skills

Narcs have no qualms telling others what an inferior parent you are. They will even tell your children. Sadly, they pull children into the mix, pretending to share things with them out of care and concern. Their goal is to make the child draw closer to them and then ultimately teach the child to disrespect you. Remember the Narc only has a limited amount of attention to give, and they assume others operate the same way. They foolishly believe the more the child loves them, the less the child will love you.

They will undermine your parenting at any given opportunity to paint themselves in a positive light. The Narc will accuse you of doing all of the very things they are guilty of in order to intentionally confuse the children and deflect. They gaslight the kids the same way that they do adults.

The Narc will not stop with the kids. They will always paint you out to be selfish, uncooperative, and unbalanced. This deflection tactic is due to their own insecurities and fear of being found out. They know that they are a lackluster parent, so if they keep the focus on you, they hope no one will take notice of how deficient they are.

They Will Demand the Children Conform to Their Unrealistic Expectations

Narcs are so obsessed with the way that they appear that they may have unrealistic expectations of their children. They don't ultimately care whether their children are happy, but rather are preoccupied that they conform to their demands for greatness. They genuinely believe that this is also for the child's own good. They believe that happiness is attained with sufficient achievements. If a child does not rise to their expectations, they are punished by the Narc. Children of Narcs can suffer from feelings of inadequacy, because no matter what they do, and how much they accomplish, they are never quite good enough in the Narc's eyes.

The Narc loves their children the same way that they do trophies or possessions, not as autonomous and sentient beings. So long as the child keeps complying with the Narc's demands and helps the Narc achieve their desired image and stature, the Narc will continue to placate the child.

They Want the Children to Love Them More

The Narc wants to win over your children in the same way they want to win over everyone else in their lives. They will resort to superficial bribes to be adored, whether this means buying the children a puppy, feeding them ice cream for dinner, or taking them to a carnival. This isn't much different from when they love bombed you in the beginning of the relationship. Narcs know how to win people over when they have something to gain. Most parents love their children's company, but Narc parents love their children's attention (and the attention from others that their children bring).

They feel empowered by controlling the children, and as a bonus, they get to inflict pain on you in the process. The Narc will constantly put the children in an untenable and unhealthy position where they have to decide which parent they love more. This is done intentionally to make themselves feel superior and create tension.

The Narc will try to out-parent you, but, like a petulant child, they lose interest in doing anything for very long. When they perceive that they have won the children over and that you are sufficiently devastated by it, they will no longer care to play the role of the perfect parent. You need to be there for your children when the Narc decides to withdraw, showing them that a parent's love is unconditional and consistent. Children can otherwise have the false impression that their worth is dependent on their behavior. They can potentially become very insecure, terrified to fall out of line, and no longer feel worthy of love.

They Envy Their Children

Most parents see their children as a reflection of themselves and want to see them succeed and do better.

They willingly make sacrifices so that their children can hopefully one day surpass them. Narc parents may look at their children like competition. They are always seeking to be the center of attention, and often children get in the way of that when they soak up the love and admiration of the room. They hate children's innocence and envy their carefree nature. If they cannot use their children to bring them attention, they will then literally compete with their children for the attention.

They Do Not Provide Emotional Support

Healthy parents provide comfort to their children and build them up. Narc parents offer no emotional refuge. They constantly put doubts in their children's heads, making them feel as though they are never enough. Regular parents are always telling their children that everything will be all right, whereas Narc parents are always planting the idea that their world is fragile and scary. It could all come crashing down at any second. Narcs never want their children to feel secure, because this may make them independent. A scared child will cling to their protector. The Narc will sadly enable dependency.

* * *

While these are the obstacles that you will face when co-parenting with a Narc, hope is not lost. There are things that you can do to make life better for you and your children, despite the adversity. Here are some tips for overcoming any potential harm done to your children as a result of the Narc's inferior parenting skills.

Focus on Your Parenting

The Narc made themselves the center of the universe for so long that it can be very difficult to not preoccupy yourself with what they are doing. You have been conditioned to constantly think about them. When they fall from grace, it's hard to switch off the obsession. You switch from thinking about appeasing them to all their nasty attributes. You start to obsess over all the horrific things the Narc does. It fills the space in your mind that is now a void. This is a terrible distraction. The focal point should always be on what you are doing, not them. Shift your focus.

You will never be able to control what the Narc does in their own home and on their own time; you can only control what goes on in your own. It is imperative to model positive attributes for your children to follow, irrespective of what your ex does. You need to make sure that your children know that you will remain by their side no matter what. You are there to protect them and ensure that they experience a healthy childhood. You cannot be with them 24/7, but you can teach your children the difference between right and wrong.

Children are incredibly perceptive. They are very quick to pick up on manipulation and bad intentions, sometimes even more so than adults. The best thing you can do for your children is to provide them with unconditional love and have them know that you are there to comfort them in anything they need.

You do not need to point out the other parent's flaws. That will be obvious on its own with time. What your children need more than anything is a role model. The best way to combat any damage done by the Narc is to teach your children what it means to love.

Do Not Speak Ill About the Other Parent

Children's self-image is comprised as being a part of each of their parents. If you speak ill about the other parent, your children may inherently feel that something is wrong with them. This is incredibly damaging to a child's psyche. Kids that feel they have a damaged parent may go through life feeling flawed and broken. Do not mistakenly send your children the message that they are broken. Children identify with both of their parents.

When children are embroiled in the middle of their parents' discord, they may try to appease both by catering to whatever either parent wants to hear. This is an unsustainable position that sends the message to the child that they are not allowed to express or feel love. They torture themselves trying to conform to their parents' conflicting demands.

You may think that you are protecting them, but warning your children about the other parent is not a good idea. Children do not need to know your former spouse's flaws. They are best served by having the healthiest relationship possible under the circumstances with both of their parents.

No matter what the Narc parent says about you, only speak about them in a laudatory way. You can and should correct misconceptions, but never insult the other parent. That will inevitably harm your child. This is incredibly difficult because the Narc will take every opportunity to make you look bad in front of your children. Resist the urge to respond in kind. It becomes very apparent which parent is hateful. You say more by remaining above the fray.

Maintain Detailed Records

Narcs consider themselves to be above the law and often fail to abide by court orders. You never know when your spouse will bring you back to court or if you will ever need the court's assistance to enforce your previously entered judgments. If your Narc constantly fails to adhere to the terms of your agreement, whether it is following a parenting time schedule or reimbursing you for the children's expenses, keep a log of their transgressions. Hopefully, you will never need to use it, but with a Narc you can never be too careful.

Narcs live in a fantasy land. They get carried away in their narratives, paying very little attention to the facts. Facts don't matter to them, because they make up reality as they go along. If they protest loudly enough, they assume their side of the story will be believed. The only way to fight their gaslighting is with tangible proof. Always hold onto the evidence.

Obtain Professional Assistance

When you and the Narc lived under the same roof, it was easy to monitor their behavior. After you part ways and live in separate homes, you have no way of gauging what the other parent is doing during their parenting time. You may not recognize what type of damage the Narc is causing your child. A mental health professional can prophylactically ensure there is nothing going on underneath the surface that needs to be addressed.

Moreover, it is important for your child to have a safe outlet to express themselves. This should be with someone other than you. A mental health professional can ensure that your child works through any underlying traumas and receives whatever support they need.

Safeguard Your Joy

In the midst of a contentious legal battle, it can become easy to succumb to your emotions and lose your joy. Be strong for the sake of your kids. They learn how to overcome challenges based on your mindset and resiliency. Ironically, shifting your attention to them will help speed along your own healing process as well.

Even if you now have to split the time you have with your children, don't let that impact the quality of the time that you have together. Less time may mean that you now have to be more intentional and present in the moments you share. Purposefully plan fun activities, go on adventures, and spend quality time together.

Do Not Partake in Any Arguments in Front of the Children

Narcs love conflict, and they know just what to say to get under your skin. Resist the urge. Children hate to see their parents argue. You want to teach them that there are healthier ways to communicate and that resorting to rude and ugly behavior is not necessary. It is best to disengage from the turmoil the Narc is trying to cause. By dismissing them, you suffocate them. Narcs know how to control the situation by creating conflict and then blaming you for the drama. By pulling away, you show your children that it is unacceptable to engage in such base and negative behavior. This does not mean that the Narc gets to say whatever they want and you passively take it. Rather, it means you do not waste your precious time trying to convince the Narc of anything. You realize that what the Narc thinks doesn't matter, and you don't waste your energy participating in a fight that has no prize.

* * *

While raising children with a Narc will undoubtedly be a challenge, it can be done. You can raise remarkable children who are caring, compassionate, and healthy, despite them having one emotionally stunted parent.

CHAPTER 11

The Smear Campaign

This is the Narc's grand finale. Their final hoorah. Once they know that you have unmasked them for who they really are, expect deliberate, preemptive retribution. They will immediately start spreading falsities about you in order to malign your character and reputation. Their approach to accepting that your relationship is over is one using scorched-earth tactics. Once the Narc no longer feels they own you, they consider it their mission to make you seem as vile and unappealing as possible. It comes down to control. If they can no longer control you, they will try to control what others think of you. As an added bonus, since you are no longer together, the worse you look, the more justified they appear in breaking away from you.

Don't forget, they are masters of triangulation, so their flying monkeys have been in place for some time. They already have a support system in place containing those who are ready to degrade you at any given moment. Plus, their gaslighting skills now can be amplified. Rather than just convincing you of falsehoods, now they can convince several people just how awful you are, while positioning themselves to be the hero in their story. Their entire life is nothing more than a screenplay in which they are the producer and lead actor. In every tale, they are either the savior or the victim. Sometimes, they are both. They can continue to curate this image by controlling the script. In doing so, they hide that they are the villain. Instead, the story they tell is that they tried to save your lost and damaged soul, but you were beyond repair.

Turning against you comes naturally to them. In their eyes, people are either fans or enemies. If you are an enemy, they are justified in taking whatever actions necessary to ensure that you remain isolated and that others lose respect for you. You are a threat to their fragile egos and the whole façade they have spent a lifetime creating. They are terrified to the core that their real selves will be exposed. They need to ensure that you lack credibility.

Their smear campaign also deflects attention away from anything you may say about them that may expose their own shortcomings. It is a diversion tactic so that your story pales in comparison. The Narc is a great storyteller and can usually one-up whatever truth you tell. They have invested so much energy in making you believe that they are infallible, that you will likely have a hard time defending yourself or speaking ill of them. You even may at times still doubt what evil they have done to you, because the cognitive dissonance from the gaslighting lingers on.

As if breaking up with the Narc wasn't hard enough, now you have to deal with this. At a time when you need to regain your confidence and have the support of those around you, the Narc continues to make you feel terrible and alone. The Narc has invested a great deal of energy in getting you to doubt yourself and isolating you from your prior social networks. Where will you go when you hit rock-bottom and have no one else to turn to? The easiest thing to do is run right back to them. The Narc is no fool. They may be evil, but in the most brilliant way. Their actions are all calculated to ensure that every door leads to coming back to them and begging for their mercy—and, more importantly, giving them even *more* control. Since they cannot control their own lives or emotions, they get off on controlling yours.

No matter how tempting it may be, you cannot respond. Do not engage the Narc directly, and do not retaliate. This is easier said than done, because the Narc will go straight to the people that matter to you the most. That is because those are the people who pose the greatest threat to the Narc.

If you react in kind, the Narc will just spin the story and embellish to make it even more heinous. They will be able to use any action you take or anything you say and twist it into proof of their side of the story. They are master manipulators who will use anything they have against you.

Their narcissistic rage will go into overdrive. They will focus all their efforts on ensuring you are miserable. These people are malevolent monsters when they feel they have been crossed. They know no bounds of decency. The best approach at this stage with the Narc is to again go grey rock. It is a lot less fun for them to spread lies about you if you don't respond or even seem to care. Those to who the Narc tells malicious lies, are less likely to believe their ridiculous tales when you remain silent. It creates a plausible deniability. Your instinct may be to react, defend yourself, and set the story straight. However, the more attention you give the story, the more credence it has.

This does not mean that you are running or hiding, but rather affirmatively deciding not to breathe any life into it. Remember how the Narc was often more powerful by saying nothing at all when they implemented the silent treatment on you? Beat them at their own game with the reverse silent treatment. Once they realize that their words are not festering away at you, the sooner they will grow weary.

The Narc is trying to get you to appear unbalanced. They want to witness you hurting from their lies. Do not give them that satisfaction. It will only prolong their campaign if they feel as though it is working. Do not condition them to know you will respond. Do not waste your precious emotional energy on something so low-based.

During this stage, many people are tempted to expose the Narc. They may try to explain to others what the Narc is doing and how deranged they are. This feat will likely be in vain. It is usually pointless to try and explain to others what is going on, as most people either won't understand or simply don't care. No matter how much they care about you, they may not care to hear about your ex's shortcomings. You so deeply want to feel understood, and you may be excited to share all that you've learned about NPD, but most of the time it is not as impactful to anyone else that has not themselves lived through it. Defending the smear campaign by trying to explain narcissism is usually a fruitless task, which may leave you appearing to be the one who is unwell to someone who does not understand the nuances.

A better course of action is to continue to move onward and upward. Focus on living a healthy and balanced life. Turn the attention away from the Narc and back onto you. Let the Narc bury themselves. With time they will paint themselves out to be the negative, vengeful, and deceptive one. They will bury themselves in their own hate.

If you fail to take the bait, they may amplify their tale of woe to try to get you to respond. The more desperate they get, the more mistakes they will make. They will expose themselves for the frauds they are. Because the Narc never says anything that is overtly nasty, the listener often does not immediately recognize the Narc to be evil. They will disguise their foul gossip as being framed in concern. They are just worried about you. However, the more times the Narc tells the story, the less objective and sincerely concerned they sound. It becomes quite evident that they are malevolent. Let them ruin their own credibility. They are good manipulators, but often weak liars. They lie so much and so often, they don't even remember the truth. People will start to pick up on the inconsistencies of their stories.

Focus on yourself and your positive relationships with others. Do not let what they say get to you, and don't feel compelled to set the record straight. Responding to the accusations often validates them. The Narc going around talking about you unilaterally makes them appear obsessed with you. You can say more in your defense by not saying anything at all.

Failing to participate in the folly does not mean that you should disappear. Quite the contrary. You should continue to be visible and live your life in its full glory. Do not run. Do not hide. Do not be ashamed of their falsehoods. Continue your life as if they do not exist. Stop letting what they say or do have any impact on you, inside or out.

Those who truly care about you cannot be taken away by the Narc. Friends and acquaintances who can be swayed were never really for you in the first place, so don't be too disappointed about their loss. The type of people who buy into this low-grade prattle are not the type of people that you want in your life moving forward.

The less impact that they see they have, the harder the Narc will try to permeate your inner circle. The Narc likely infiltrated your family back in the early stages of the relationship. They made themselves close to your loved ones while isolating you from them. They may continue to feign interest in your loved ones after the relationship concludes so that they can continue to divide and conquer, control the narrative, and separate you from your support structure. They still desire to get information about you from those who are on the inside. The more they know, the more they can weave into their stories. Meanwhile, you feel betrayed and as though no matter how hard you try, you cannot escape them. Do not allow the Narc the satisfaction of compromising any of your relationships. Carry on as you always have. Live your life unphased by the Narc's attempts to sequester you from your social circle.

The Narc will tell anyone who will listen about their saga of suffering. They will gladly talk to your neighbors. If they have any inroads, they will also likely go to your employer and colleagues. They want to ensure that every environment you are in is hostile and that you have no refuge. The Narc never feels safe. They live in constant fear of being exposed for the monster they really are and this is why they want you to feel this same pain. They know how insufferable it can be.

The smear campaign hurts the most when you share children with the Narc and the Narc tries to turn the kids against you. They invariably will do so. They will immediately

CHAPTER 11 ■ THE SMEAR CAMPAIGN

become the fun parent. They will buy the children's affection with puppies, candy for dinner, any toy they desire, a trip to the amusement park, and fail to set any boundaries during their parenting time. They will convince the children that *you* are the reason for the family's destruction. It doesn't matter what is written in any court order or how much it damages the children; as long as the Narc is hurting you, they consider their false narratives to be worth the cost of admission.

While you are in court against the Narc, the smear campaign will escalate to an all-time high. If the Narc can turn those closest to you against you, imagine what they can do to strangers. The Narc can charm and manipulate their way into the hearts of the judge, mediator, and attorneys (even your own). Don't be surprised if the Narc makes some outlandish allegations, buries you in paperwork, says things that they know will hurt you to the core, and asks for things they don't really want (simply because they know you do).

No matter how the Narc tells the story, and to whom, one thing in the story will always remain the same: that they are the tragic victim. You were beyond repair. They tried to fix you. You took advantage of them. They miss you but need to stay away. The particulars of the story will vary in each and every situation. Maybe you are a thief, liar, gold digger, psychopath, cheater, abuser, drinker, or addict. Whatever it is, they have been trying to protect you from yourself for so long. It will certainly contain an element of questioning your mental and emotional well-being. They have to make sure that if you speak ill about them, the listener will cast doubts on anything that you say, because they believe you are so damaged.

In order to not seem as though they are spreading rumors or have malicious intent, they will characterize the negative things they say about you under the cloak of concern. To be sure that it is believable, the story will have little elements of truth sprinkled throughout, things that people can confirm and know to be true. That way the listener can validate the tale. After they have the other person hooked, they begin to embellish. Never underestimate how ridiculous or far-fetched the story can be. It creates the drama and intrigue that they thrive on. Plus, it keeps people coming back to them for more information.

The Narc feeds off of people listening to their fables. Now they are, yet again, the center of attention. This makes them even more relentless. They will tell anyone who will listen. They continue to fuel the story and keep it alive because it keeps them relevant—and tortures you. To deflect, they accuse you of the very things that they themselves have done to you. That way, if you allege the same thing in your defense, your story will seem less credible.

There are no boundaries with the Narc. They will share even the most intimate communications, photos, or videos to ensure that you are the outcast. The entire time they were love bombing you, they were on an investigative mission. They studied you so that they could understand what made you the most vulnerable and tried to get you to open up and share your deepest and darkest secrets. These are the things that they will use against you in the smear campaign. They will use what they have, and if they don't have enough, they'll make it up. Narcs actually believe their own lies. While they carry on acting in such a deranged manner, they actually do convince themselves that you are the villain. Their goal is to devastate you for daring to expose the fact that they are not endowed with the godlike power that they believe they possess.

The Narc will do anything necessary to maintain their delusion of a superior self. Whatever collateral damage they cause to you is absolutely irrelevant to them. They will not come to their senses, and they will not regret what they say or do. You cannot reason with them. Do not try.

You should know that the smear campaign started long before the discard. Even when you were in the love bombing stage, the Narc was behind the scenes planting seeds of discord amongst others towards you. It would seem all too contrived if you were the perfect love interest and then suddenly become a raving lunatic overnight. It is a slow buildup. They consistently create a momentum in their stories, leading up to you being cruel and unstable. In their warped minds, it's even fun.

The smear campaign is inevitable. How far they will go typically depends on whether you engage them. You took the best action you could against it when you decided to end your relationship with an abuser. No matter how much the Narc detests you, they never want you to be free of them. They look at you as a trophy that they conquered. By keeping the controversy alive, they stay connected to you and feed their need for control. No matter how tempting it may seem, do not negotiate with a terrorist.

CHAPTER 12

Healing And Recovery

One of the strangest things about narcissistic abuse is that even when you realize that the other person is a monster, you still miss them. You grieve the loss and try to find some way to rationalize, excuse, and justify their behavior. It is a sick and twisted web that you got wrapped up in, and it is not easy to break the Stockholm Syndrome. Trauma bonds can often outlast the relationship. The intense highs and lows that you experienced while the two of you were together leave a void when suddenly gone. While you feel a sense of peace, you simultaneously fear the unknown. You start to crave the cycle of wounding and soothing as you associate it with healing. You are not actually bonded to the person, but to the cycle of abuse.

Every evil thing they did to you was intentional. They cheated because they felt like it. They made you cry because it made them feel powerful. They abandoned you to watch you crawl after them. They broke you so that they could feel godlike. If that's not looking into the face of evil, then I don't know what is.

You may be wondering: How long it will take for you to get over the Narc? I am not going to sugarcoat it. Many people never do. They live their lives bitter, angry, and resentful. They refuse to trust and love again. Instead, they wallow in their pity and sour those around them. They blame every bad thing that happens to them in their lives moving forward as somehow stemming from the Narc—no matter how far removed.

Do not turn into this person. This is the path of least resistance: Victimization takes over your life. You have lost all inspiration. Nothing excites you. You become addicted to the hurt. You have spent so much time in pain that you have become comfortable there. You tell people about how rotten your ex is. How they used you and abused you. How you have nothing left. Your friends grow tired of listening to it. You fall deeper into the abyss.

It's not your heart that is hurting; it is your mind. You can't shut it off. It is on a loop where you are reliving the trauma and questioning every action you took since the inception of the relationship. The memories flood back in, and it feels as though you are drowning. It's okay to grieve. You were a victim. You experienced something evil. That is the truth. However, you can overcome this negative experience. You can grow better from it. People can rise above bad circumstances and use them to better themselves and others.

It is just as easy to channel that pain into a healthy outlet as it is to sink into depression. If you are going through a difficult time, at least make it productive. Position yourself in a manner that moves you further towards the vision of who you had always hoped you would be. You need to reframe your purpose. Adversity is an opportunity that you can use to launch yourself into the next phase of your life.

To move forward, sometimes you must go backward. It's counterintuitive, but you must remind yourself of who you are at a very primal and basic level. Who were you before you met the Narc? What made you feel alive? Go back to find your former self in order to determine who you want to become in the future. What advice would the old you give your current self? What was the old you on the path to becoming? Do not lose sight of your authentic self. You almost need to erase that period of time you were with the Narc. While denial is generally a bad thing, you may need to momentarily suspend reality and pretend that the Narc had never entered your life. Where were you heading? Keep going there.

The Narc was nothing but a roadblock. Even if they have been with you for decades, or a majority of your life, it is still just a slice. You experienced good things in life before them, and you will experience good things in life after them. The Narc was a chapter. You are the author. You are what makes the story beautiful, and you get to decide whether there is a happy ending.

How long it ultimately takes you to get over it is completely up to you. You do not need to wait for some sort of external event. If you are always waiting for the right time, you will be waiting forever. Nothing comes into your life and suddenly makes you happy. Contentment always starts from within. You make the conscious decision to wake up and start your day from a place of positivity. Your frame of mind is not solely dependent on your circumstances. Happiness is a choice, not an event.

You cannot be joyful all the time, but you can find something to be grateful for during every moment you are on this earth. Certainly, bad things can and will happen, and you may be perfectly justified to experience periods of sadness and anger, but you cannot reside there. Negativity should be a temporary state, not a default way of life. Shift your focus. Ending things with the Narc is really just a new beginning.

You have nothing to lose by making a deliberate effort to pursue joy. If it doesn't work out, you can still go right back to being morose. Give optimism a chance. Start each morning by acknowledging the wonderful things that you have and the things that are to come. Your state of mind when you begin your day has a major impact on how the rest of your day goes. If you wake up anxious, you will continue to become more fraught as the day proceeds. If you wake up excited, opportunities will follow. You attract things that parallel your state of mind. Imagine the possibilities when you are receptive to joy. For too many years, you allowed the Narc to be your frame of reference. They no longer get to decide what you do or how you feel.

Many people who have been in a long-term relationship with a Narc suffer from decision-paralysis. They are so used to the Narc controlling their lives that they don't feel comfortable making decisions for themselves. They have constantly been told that they are wrong and that their thinking is faulty. As a result, they doubt their choices. This timidity leads to an indecisiveness that ultimately leads to stagnation and depression.

If you have been with a Narc long enough, you turn into a confused squirrel about to cross the road, unable to successfully make even the most benign decisions. You want to move, but you hesitate. You see danger. You cannot decide what to do. Indecisiveness has a price. Do not allow yourself to become a flat squirrel. The more you question yourself, the more prone you are to making poor decisions. Commit to moving forward with your life and leaving the past behind.

The longer the relationship lasted, the deeper the trauma. Some people never heal because they have no idea where to begin. You do not have to have your whole life planned out to take the first step towards a better future. Take decisive action that you are cutting the Narc out like a cancer. Be grateful that you have been given a second chance at life. Once you commit to removing the Narc, vow to making yourself stronger. This may feel impossible in the moment, but do it anyway. Continue to become who you dreamed of becoming, whether you feel like it or not. You cannot wait for the perfect moment to start healing. Go through the motions, and the healing will follow.

The Narc is damaged beyond repair. They are so broken that they have to take everyone in their path down with them in order to make themselves feel human. Be better than the Narc. Heal yourself; otherwise, you will unconsciously also hurt those around you.

Even for those who successfully turn their lives around for the better post-Narc, there are going to be some very dark and trying times. The trauma does not evaporate in a nanosecond. You will experience a cyclical healing process where things will feel hopeless, and then there is light. This pattern will repeat a number of times until eventually the lows aren't quite as extreme and don't occur quite as often.

It is often said that it takes twenty-one days to create a habit and ninety days to reinvent your life. My experience tells me that for a normal, healthy adult who was truly in love with and devastated by a Narc, that it is going to take at least a year and probably is not really going to fully lift until you fall in love again. Most people don't want to hear this harsh reality. A year seems like a lifetime. Falling in love again sounds impossible. Be that as it may, it is the truth. You need to experience all holidays and special events at least once without their presence. You need to fall in love with yourself again. Eventually, after you have done those things, you can begin to open your heart to the idea of loving someone new.

Before that, you need to grieve. You cannot turn your emotions on and off without facing the hurt. The loss of the Narc is not just the loss of a partner; it's realizing that you lost yourself. Processing that takes time. One day the fog will clear. You will wake up from the nightmare. The shock will eventually wear off, and you will realize that you experienced evil in its most raw and pure form. You were addicted and entrenched in a cult. Addictions do not cure themselves overnight.

Once you cease all communications with the Narc and start reuniting yourself with family and friends, you slowly start to become more aware of what was happening to you. Even though you know you were in a bad situation, you cannot fully appreciate the insanity of it all until you start to tell other people about your relationship. When you talk about your relationship out loud, you'll realize that you were living in prison, held by your own free will, alongside the most sadistic guard.

If you want to know how to beat a Narc, the answer is very simple: You already did. You don't beat them in the courtroom. You beat them in your mind. You walk away. Forever. You don't allow them to inflict any more pain. You don't give them the pleasure of getting any reaction from you, good or bad. You find your joy again.

If you are reading this book, you already won. You identified the Narc. You did your homework, and you ended the cycle. You made a decision that you would not condone their rotten behavior any longer. As a result, the Narc feels irrelevant. A lack of attention, significance, and control are their deepest fears. You cut off all their supply and caused them narcissistic injury. This is the greatest pain, because it invalidates their existence and causes emotional annihilation. They know that they no longer have any control over you.

Moving on with your life destroys the Narc. Do not be motivated by revenge; rather, you should be motivated by your own success. You will know that you have finally gotten over the Narc when you look back and see that they never actually had anything to offer. It was you that brought so much to the relationship. Narcs only pair themselves with those who they see as strong and independent.

Many victims struggle to focus on themselves again. They have been programmed to spend their lives serving the Narc, so they do not even know what it is like to meet their own needs anymore. Narcs make their partners feel guilty for experiencing any joy or success in their presence. This conditioning can lead to the fear of making any decisions or taking bold independent moves without the Narc's input or blessing.

You may hide your gifts and talents after being brainwashed that you are for some unexplainable reason not good enough. Maybe they convinced you that pursuing your passions makes you selfish. The Narc intentionally depleted you of your autonomy. They created a dependency that left you hostage. Don't doubt yourself. You are exceptional, and that is why the Narc was drawn to you in the first place.

A broken heart is painful, but a broken spirit is debilitating. The depth of this wound is a thousand times deeper than any breakup you've ever had to deal with before. You are not mending a broken heart; you are repairing a shattered soul. This feels different because it *is* different. True love does not make you feel as though you need to hide and change. True love makes you feel like you are prized and desired. The more of you, the better. The Narc made you bury yourself so deep that you struggle to find yourself again.

Do not wait any longer to move on. You need to accept that you will never get the closure you so desperately crave. The Narc will always leave the door open to reenter your life, and they intentionally leave you confused. The closest you can get to an explanation is to understand the intricacies of NPD. Learning about the nuances of Narcs, and how they are all the same, is cathartic. You may find yourself addicted to learning about this disease. Even referring to NPD as a "disease," though, seems like a cop-out. It implies that the host has no control. The Narc is no victim. They are painfully and gloriously aware of what they are doing. They have no desire to change or get better.

If you allow the Narc the opportunity to explain, you are only setting yourself up for heartache. They will use each and every one of your words against you. You will start to doubt yourself again. They are master manipulators. They know the precise answers you want to hear, and they will appease you, but just enough to make you receptive to giving them yet another chance.

If someone leaves you in the dirt, plant a seed and grow. Bury them in their own emotional void. You will never realize how much it destroys the Narc to know that you have moved on. It does not feel like the satisfying revenge that you so desperately crave. Yet it is the deepest wound you can ever inflict on the Narc's fragile ego. By making them feel insignificant, you destroy them, and in turn you develop a better self.

The crazy part is that even if you know beyond a doubt that the Narc is a toxic force in your life, you will still initially feel terrified at the prospect of being alone. Once you realize you were alone all along, you will at first become depressed, but with time, you will become liberated. If you got over the person who you once loved the most abusing you, you can get through anything. In that solitude and reflection, you will find grace, mercy, and strength. You will realize that you are healing and that there is a lot of beauty in this world. Go chase it. Go create it. Go experience it.

You need to be just as thankful for your closed doors as for your open ones. You cannot always reopen a door that has been shut, but you can decide which one to open next. Do not get stuck. Keep moving forward whether you feel like it or not. Immediately following the loss of the Narc, you will lack happiness. Keep moving forward anyway. Your future self will thank you. It is okay to start over: Sometimes by choice. Sometimes by force. Whatever the reason, every new beginning is an opportunity as much as it is a challenge.

Naturally you're going to wonder time from time... *How is the Narc? What are they doing? Are they happy?* In order to heal, you need to completely stop yourself from thinking of them. It is hard. Especially when your whole life used to cater around their well-being.

If you really want to know what the Narc is doing, it's the same thing. The Narc is going through the motions of the things that you experienced together, but now with someone else. They are probably taking their new paramour to dinner at the same restaurants and going on the same trips. Narcs gets a sick and twisted joy out of reliving the same experiences with different actors. Eventually, the new victim will go through the exact same rollercoaster ride through Hades.

The Narc may have replaced you with their secondary supply or perhaps they turned to social media to find a completely new pool of people altogether. Narcs love social media. It feeds the part of their soul that needs attention but lacks depth. No matter who they have cast for the role, you can pretty much guarantee they are doing the same things that they always have. Narcs are creatures of habit. They soothe themselves by going back to experiences that have served them well in the past. By living their life on repeat, they feel safe and in control of the situation.

The Narc doesn't get to experience a happy ending, though. They may appear to have it all on the outside. For a brief period in their lives, they often really do. They tend to be high-wage earners. They find people who genuinely care about them. They live the perfect life on social media. However, as they get older, they can't help but ruin every good thing around them. Misery is their natural state. Building a façade is the only thing they know. The older they get, the more their house of cards crumbles. They get divorced. They acquire debts to appear as though they have more assets. For sport, they beat down those who genuinely care for them. As they age, they often find themselves alone and exposed as the frauds they truly are.

At the end of the day, though, it does not matter what the Narc is doing or what happened to them. As difficult as it is, you need to focus completely on you. Give yourself permission to be selfish. The key to recovery from narcissistic abuse is ironically turning all of the attention from them back onto yourself.

You need to reform your identity. It is time to get excited, reinvigorated, and reenergized about becoming the person you wanted to become before the Narc entered your life. You are not going to feel it for a while. Go through the motions anyways. The depression and loss will follow you around like a heavy cloud, but one day it will vanish, and when it does you want to awake from the smog and find yourself further ahead. You can't wait to heal before you start taking action to rebuild your life; the healing will naturally occur in the process.

The only way to recover is to reinvent yourself. New habits. New people. New dreams. Sometimes to find the new, you may need to go back to the basics. Just like there was a cycle to narcissistic abuse, there is a cycle to narcissistic recovery. It takes an inordinate amount of work to get over this type of emotional warfare, but if you want to, you will prevail. You get to decide when you are over it.

As impossible as it may seem, you can regain the peace and optimism you once had. Know that everyone takes a different amount of time to heal. It may take years to get over it. Do not lose hope because you feel it is taking longer than it should. Relationships with Narcs take longer to get over because we do not ever leave on our own terms. We leave because we know it's the only thing we can do to save ourselves.

Take the trauma that you experienced and use it to rebuild a better, stronger, more organic version of your authentic self. One that is completely impermeable by anyone else's words and actions. Do not waste the pain. This hurt that you have pent up inside you is energy that can be transformed into something beautiful. You often hear of artists creating their best works out of their tragedies. It may sound crazy, but the hurt that is bottled up can be used in a meaningful way. Extreme joy and extreme pain both can be used as a source of passion. Harness it.

Once you have taken some time to focus on yourself and start rebuilding a new life, you need to find an outlet to redirect the love you have to give. Go adopt a kitten or a puppy. You desperately need some unconditional love. Volunteer somewhere meaningful to help others who are less fortunate. Whatever you do, do not immediately throw yourself into another relationship, because your mental state may make you vulnerable to another Narc waltzing their way into your life. I am not suggesting you should be afraid of love, or that everyone is like this, but you need to focus on recovery before re-immersion.

You will be a better partner and ultimately be more satisfied in your future relationships by taking the time to put yourself in a healthy frame of mind before reconnecting. Otherwise, you risk falling back into a codependent state. It's hard not to look for love when you are feeling scared and alone. You are so used to catering to the Narc's needs that you'll have a desire to fill this void with someone new. If you try to move on too quickly, you risk replacing the Narc with someone who wants to take advantage of your kindness.

One of the best things you can do to move forward from the experience is to write your story. Diary your narrative. One of the nastiest side effects of the gaslighting is how you will continue to doubt your mind even long after the Narc is gone. There will be days you wake up confused and wonder if you caused it all. You didn't. You may doubt your memory, but you'll be less inclined to doubt your written experiences.

The outside world may trivialize what you went through. Your recollection will become distorted with time (naturally, as it does for everyone as time passes). Don't forget. Put it all on paper while it's still fresh. Write down the facts. Write down how it made you feel. Putting it in a tangible form will not make it any clearer in the beginning, but I assure you that with time you will find clarity. Get the feelings you had for the Narc out of your head and dump these thoughts onto some tangible medium. Then try to forget about all of it the best you can and for as long as you can. Sometimes if you unload your thoughts onto paper, you can let go of reliving them because you know they live somewhere else. It's strange, but you may fear forgetting. You are afraid that if you let go of the pain, you will inadvertently also erase the good. Even though forgetting is precisely what you need to do to move forward. Let it go.

Healing from trauma is a very unique and subjective experience. While for most people, writing it down and tucking it away is healthy, for others, they may need to

HOW TO DIVORCE A NARCISSIST AND WIN ■ MARIE SARANTAKIS

watch the videos and look at the photos. If you find yourself reminiscing and missing the way the Narc made you feel, go through your phone. Think about your state of mind during each of these occasions. You were often a mess, weren't you? Sure, there may have been moments of euphoria. Like the moments you actually got the Narc to confess their undying love and devotion to you; but those moments were brief and were likely surrounded by a lot of agony and grief. Some people heal by directly confronting and experiencing the pain. They need to go through it again in their minds in order to get over it.

Others cope with this loss through denial. They cannot deal with the pain or replaying the tragic moments over and over in their head. They move on by pretending as though that period of time did not exist.

However you decide to cope with the pain, you need to ensure that it is limited in time. The grief should not be prolonged. Deal with it as you deem best and then move forward. You need to accept that you have removed yourself from a situation that was no longer serving you. Not because you were weak, but because you were strong. It became a matter of life and death, and you chose life. You had the faith that you could do better and start anew. You believed in yourself more than you believed in your captor.

The person that you thought you knew and loved is dead. In fact, they never existed in the first place. They were a hologram of what you projected. In each and every relationship, the Narc is a chameleon, becoming an entirely new being to appease their then partner's dreams and desires. How can you mourn the loss of someone who was faking the core of their character? You can only mourn the *idea* of them, which was a figment of both of your collective imaginations. It was a fantasy that came to a crashing and unexplainable end.

One day you'll grow to appreciate this chapter. The Devil sent to destroy you launched you into the next and most beautiful stage of your life. You can either see the loss of the Narc as a void or as a space full of endless possibilities. Now you know exactly what you want your future to look like. You have the most life experience behind you that you have ever had, and you can create real and sustainable magic. While it may have felt like it, you never experienced real love. You experienced a cheap substitute, loaded with infatuation and fantasy. Real love makes you a stronger version of yourself. The other person loves your authenticity. Meanwhile a Narc resents you and systematically works to destroy your uniqueness.

When you finally do recover, it will seem as though you have awoken from a long slumber. You'll be disoriented and feel confused by even the simplest of tasks that you used to enjoy. If you have had a Narc in your life long enough, you began to erode. All that is left is a shell of your former being, and you feel like you need to get to know yourself again. It may surprise you to learn that in order to get revenge on the Narc, you start by loving yourself again. You take that energy you focused on them, and you channel it back towards yourself.

You may envy the Narc. It must be nice to be so cold and indifferent. In the middle of the pain, you will wish you could be so callous and disconnected from your feelings. You think it would be a gift to have been spared the pain of loss. However, the truth is that you should be grateful for every tear you shed. There is a beauty in the hurt. It means that you are capable of love. You made a sacrifice for another human being. Don't let the fact that they betrayed you stop you from loving again. Don't let it make you bitter. You are the lucky one. You felt something. You are real. You will feel something again. The Narc is completely incapable of loving someone else, and they are incapable of loving themselves.

The Narc is broken beyond repair. Do not let them break you. You danced with the Devil, and you now have a chance to walk away. Take it. Once you have come out of the fire and have cleaned up the ashes, you will realize that you have survived something that very few people have. You were broken, and you rebuilt. You began anew. You defeated more than a monster; you defeated Lucifer himself. You no longer fear hell. You visited and picked up a souvenir. Now be grateful that you no longer reside there.

No matter how painful the healing process may be, appreciate the good times that you had. The truth is that there is no high like that when the Narc was love bombing you. You experienced love, even if they didn't. Maybe it was just a mirage, but at times it sure felt amazing. It was real to you. Their inability to love you back was not because you were unworthy of being loved; it was because they did not know how. All the love you gave them and felt in your heart was pure. Take joy in knowing that one day you will give that love to someone else, and it will feel even more amazing when it is real and reciprocated.

When you walk away from anything in your past, whether good or bad, you can either appreciate it for what it was or be filled with regret. I encourage you to be grateful. There is the old inquiry: whether it is better to have loved and lost or to have never loved at all. In time, you will see that the pain was worth the pleasure. The memories were worth the tears. And you are worth so much more than you can ever imagine.

If you take nothing else away from this book, I hope you know the following: This was not your fault, and there is nothing you could have done to fix them or to salvage the relationship. You are a beautiful person, and that is why they tried so hard to destroy you.

The only way to get even with the Narc is to live your best life ever.

You are at a crossroads. It's up to you where you go next.

After the end of every chapter, you have a choice. The experience can make you better, or it can make you bitter. Life is not something that happens to you, it is something you create. Socrates once said, "The secret of change is to focus all of your energy not on fighting the old, but on building the new." Let your lawyer do the fighting.

Go out there. Start anew. Live. Love. Flourish.

ABOUT THE AUTHOR

Marie Sarantakis is a prominent family law attorney, best-selling author, and nationally recognized divorce coach. As a high-profile litigator, she is intimately familiar with how narcissistic personality disorder impacts divorce cases and how to gain a strategic advantage in the courtroom. As a coach, she helps those who are recovering from narcissistic abuse find their joy and purpose. To learn more about Marie Sarantakis, visit www.mariesarantakis.com.

Made in the USA
Columbia, SC
24 September 2022

67882811R00111